Minecraft®
Basics

by Jesse Stay, Joseph Stay, and Alexander Stay

T0049583

for
dummies®

A Wiley Brand

Minecraft® Basics For Dummies®

Published by: **John Wiley & Sons, Inc.**, 111 River Street, Hoboken, NJ 07030-5774, www.wiley.com

Copyright © 2022 by John Wiley & Sons, Inc., Hoboken, New Jersey

Published simultaneously in Canada

For general information on our other products and services, please contact our Customer Care Department within the U.S. at 877-762-2974, outside the U.S. at 317-572-3993, or fax 317-572-4002. For technical support, please visit www.wiley.com/techsupport.

Wiley publishes in a variety of print and electronic formats and by print-on-demand. Some material included with standard print versions of this book may not be included in e-books or in print-on-demand. If this book refers to media such as a CD or DVD that is not included in the version you purchased, you may download this material at http://booksupport.wiley.com. For more information about Wiley products, visit www.wiley.com.

Library of Congress Control Number: 2022944079

ISBN: 978-1-119-90748-0 (pbk); ISBN 978-1-119-90749-7 (ebk); ISBN 978-1-119-90750-3 (ebk)

SKY10034729_082322

Contents at a Glance

Table of Contents

Introduction

I f you enjoy games about building, survival, engineering, or adventuring, the game of Minecraft is for you. Having attracted more than 141 million monthly active players (and selling 238 million copies at the time we wrote this book), it is the most-often-downloaded game on the Internet — and it's the most widely used metaverse (an online, immersive and simulated digital world, played by real humans) ever created. Minecraft is a loose-ended yet adventurous sandbox game that becomes whatever you make of it.

As a family of two divorced coparents and seven kids, we all quickly became aware of the influence that Minecraft has on families — together or apart. When the kids would invite their friends over, and after all of them were engrossed in using a tablet or a Kindle device, they would explore and play and sometimes nag each other in the game. "Dad, Alex just blew up my house!" is a common phrase in our household.

Perhaps, in your own family structure or with the kids in your life, you've seen a similar situation, wondering what in the world these kids are talking about and whether you should be concerned. Or perhaps you're one of the children who is playing and you want to better understand how to build the largest village or automate your entire world by using farms, iron golems, or even redstone contraptions and circuitry. This benefit has led to most of the older children in our family developing an interest in, and even competing in, FIRST Robotics League, where they build real-life robots in high school.

Minecraft is all about gathering resources and building structures while facing monsters. The world of Minecraft is composed of cubic blocks, which you can break and replace to build houses and craft items — that's all there is to it. The game has evolved to become so balanced and complex that it has attracted hundreds of millions of satisfied fans. While skimming or scouring *Minecraft Basics For Dummies,* you can apply every bit of Minecraft information you need to start playing the game to your liking.

About This Book

We wrote this book as a family. Jesse is the dad; Joseph is the 17-year-old in college a year early, some of that due to his experience playing Minecraft as a kid; and (in the position held by Joseph in the previous edition of this book, *Minecraft For Dummies*) his 11-year-old younger brother, Alex, with icons labeled throughout this book from his perspective. And Thomas, the now 20-year-old, wrote most of the previous edition of this book! This book was a family project, and our hope is that other families and family-type units can benefit from this book, just as we have.

This book, in a sense, operates much like Minecraft does: After you have the basic ingredients, you can take your game wherever you want. Skip to The End. Advance to the Nether. Just pick a chapter and start reading.

Take this book and share it with a close friend. Let your parents read it. Let your children or the kids in your life read it. Share it with a school classroom. Invite us to join you. (Just email minecraft@staynalive.com and we'll give it our best!) Minecraft, whether it's played with friends or the mobs in your own single-player virtual world, is truly a social experience and is best played with people you know. We hope that you can share the knowledge in this book with the same people you play with in the game.

Foolish Assumptions

Minecraft continually releases new updates and features — this book is accurate to Minecraft version 1.18. Because later Minecraft updates are unlikely to change the primary game mechanics, this book encompasses most of Minecraft's main features. Check out our *Minecraft For Dummies* YouTube channel at www.youtube.com/minecraftdummiesbook, where we'll address any future updates to Minecraft, or the Minecraft Wiki at http://Minecraft.gamepedia.com, if you ever have questions not addressed in this book.

Rather than try to consider every single type of reader who might pick up this book, we've made certain assumptions about you, the reader:

>> You have a computer or mobile device (or, optionally, your favorite gaming console), and you know how to use it.

>> You know what a web browser is, and you can surf the web.

>> You have an email address, and you know how to use it.

>> Your computer can download and run Java programs.

>> You have a functioning keyboard and computer mouse.

Icons Used in This Book

We've placed various icons in the margins of this book to point out specific information that you may find useful:

TIP

This icon calls attention to any tip or trick that you can use to enhance the gameplay.

ALEX'S CORNER

These tips, written by Joseph's 11-year-old brother, Alex, reflect the mindset of the younger generation of Minecraft players (11 years and younger).

REMEMBER

This icon emphasizes information that you should attempt to retain in your memory. If you can remember these special points, you'll become a better player.

WARNING

If you see this icon, read its information! Warnings can prevent you from making a big mistake that can be hazardous to your Minecraft world (or your computer). We don't want you to learn these lessons the hard way — like we undoubtedly did.

TECHNICAL STUFF

You can safely skip this geeky stuff. However, it deserved a place in the book, so you may be interested in reading it.

Conventions Used in This Book

In *Minecraft Basics For Dummies,* we use numbered steps, bullet lists, and screen shots for your reference. We also provide a few sidebars containing information that's nonessential but may help you understand a topic a little better. Web addresses appear in a special monotype font that looks like this:

```
www.youtube.com/minecraftdummiesbook
```

Beyond the Book

Understanding Minecraft goes beyond these pages and onto the Internet, where you can access additional information:

>> **Cheat Sheet:** You can find this book's online Cheat Sheet at www.dummies.com/extras/minecraft.

You also can follow this book's YouTube channel, as well as the book's Facebook Page. We've also set up a Facebook Group for you to collaborate with, and learn from, each other. Here's how to find them all:

>> *Minecraft For Dummies* **YouTube channel:** https:// youtube.com/minecraftdummiesbook

>> *Minecraft For Dummies* **Facebook Page:** https:// facebook.com/minecraftfd

>> *Minecraft For Dummies* **Facebook Group:** https:// facebook.com/groups/minecraftfordummies

More than anything, get out there and play Minecraft. We hope to see you sometime — look under the username jessestay for Jesse, TheRealStayman for Thomas, expelymarndo for Joseph, and Alex_Stay for Alex. See you in the Nether!

1

Getting Started with Minecraft

Chapter **1**

Minecraft Is for Everyone — But What Is It?

inecraft is what you make of it. It can be a complete waste of time, or it can be a place to learn, explore, create, and compete — at all ages and coming from various backgrounds. I wrote an entire book about it, *with* my kids! It's not just for kids. Minecraft is for everyone!

Although the rest of the book is coauthored by my son, Joseph, with some tips interspersed by another of my children, Alex, this chapter has been written entirely by me, the dad, who's familiar with the concerns of parenting a Minecraft "Steve" or "Alex" — which are the names of the default male and female characters everyone assumes when they begin to play Minecraft.

I, Jesse's 11-year-old son, am named Alex, but in addition to "Steve," who identifies as he/him and is a boy in the game, you can also choose to start as a she/her girl character named "Alex" in the game. Don't get me confused with the default girl Minecraft character, though, when you read the "Alex's Corners."

When my friends and other parental figures find out that I helped write the book *Minecraft For Dummies* with my children, I'm usually flooded with millions of questions: "What is Minecraft?" "Is it safe for children?" "My kids are always on Minecraft — isn't it a waste of time?" "I need your book! Will you sign a copy for me?"

I always smile whenever they ask that last question. I hope that you're one of these people, and that I, and my kids, have signed your book.

The truth is that Minecraft is an amazing teaching tool and a product that every parent can use to encourage exploratory learning, where children get to explore new concepts in a controlled environment.

Playing Minecraft with the Children in Your Life

The best thing you can do in Minecraft as a parent, coparent, guardian, or that favorite uncle or aunt for the kids in your life is play with them. They'll bond with you in ways you never anticipated, and you'll get to know the game — *and* find new ways to teach the kids by using the game. Minecraft is an excellent educational tool for kids, and the gameplay is full of opportunities for parental figures and teachers to participate in the learning process. I personally — as a single, divorced coparent — enjoy using the game as a way to bond remotely with my kids when they aren't at my house and they're with their mom instead.

Rather than refer you to Chapter 2 to get started, I present a few highlights and cross-references in this section so that you can hit the ground running with the kids in *your* life.

Getting a handle on the basics

Peruse the official Minecraft wiki at `https://minecraft.fandom.com`. It has up-to-date information about Minecraft — more than you've ever wanted to know. Ads and downloads that are available on the wiki can introduce malware to your computer if you're not careful, so consider letting your kids focus on the information in this book and reserving the wiki for yourself.

Minecraft has two main modes: Creative and Survival. In Survival mode, you can still play with other players, but dangerous mobs abound (usually, evil characters that can kill you) and you can die (see Figure 1-1). If you play in Survival mode, check out the section in Chapter 3 about setting up for your first night. Few people survive the first night on their first attempt.

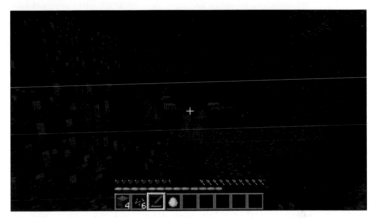

FIGURE 1-1: A hostile mob in Minecraft.

If you truly want to play the game and dodge evil, Survival mode might be for you. But if you simply want to explore and learn by playing with your kids, try out Creative mode, as explained in the following section.

Playing in Creative mode

In Creative mode in Minecraft, you can truly do anything you want without having to risk dying — in this mode, nothing can kill you except yourself. And you have access to almost every resource in order to build anything you want. And you can even fly!

To get started in Creative mode, you can either select it as you start gameplay (see Figure 1-2) or, within Survival mode, if cheats are enabled, type **/gamemode creative** and it automatically switches to Creative mode. Refer to Chapter 2 to see what you can do within Creative mode.

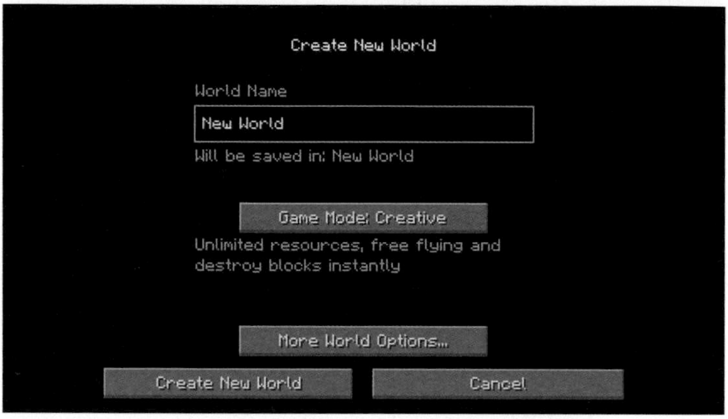

FIGURE 1-2: Selecting Creative mode as you start Minecraft.

Winning the game

After you've had some practice in Creative mode, you can start playing in Survival mode to win the game — though the truth is that you never actually win the game. Minecraft is a *sandbox* game: It has no true beginning or end, so the focus of the game is entirely on exploring, and on surviving, as you explore the game.

You'll want to achieve some initial goals, however, as described in the following list, before you move on to plain ol' exploration (refer to Chapter 11 for details on each step).

Letting Minecraft Help You Teach

I asked my sons, Joseph and Alex (and before that, Thomas, in the previous edition) to write most of this book because I wanted them to be the ones to show me what topics pique their interest and to explain why those topics are interesting to them. If you spend some time reading the chapters in this book, you'll quickly realize that Minecraft is much more than a silly-looking game.

In fact, I mentioned this to one of my children's schoolteachers and they invited my children to come talk about Minecraft to their class, for this very reason! Minecraft lets you explore an entire world where you experience life by engaging in these types of activities:

>> **Mining and geography/geology:** The sole premise of Minecraft is that you dig into your world's natural resources and gather different types of stone, precious metals, ore, and wood in order to build and create structures, as shown in Figure 1-3. The more you mine, the more you can build and create.

FIGURE 1-3: The first concept that your kids explore in Minecraft is likely to be geology and the process of mining to "create" structures.

Kids can quickly see that certain types of metal and stone cut faster than others. Wood can burn if placed near a flame or lava. Lava lurks deep within the earth. And dangerous creatures roam among the trees and plants!

>> **Farming:** Our family announced our latest pregnancy by taking a screen shot of a pink sheep and a blue sheep that had just produced a random pink sheep. (Yes, it was a girl. See Figure 1-4 to see the announcement.) In Minecraft farming, you get to learn about the birds and the bees by viewing animals in 8-bit format — a format that's safe for young kids to view (and fun, too).

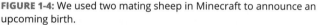

Minecraft Recipes For Dummies
Posted by Jesse Stay [?] · September 27

It's a girl! Thomas and family are getting a new little sister: — with Jesse Stay.

Like · Comment · Share · Buffer · Assign To   ⤻ 1 Share

FIGURE 1-4: We used two mating sheep in Minecraft to announce an upcoming birth.

On a Minecraft farm, you learn about growing plants and about needing to water plants to make them grow. You learn about preventing pests and other creatures that can harm your plants and animals. You also learn that the meat you eat comes from real-life animals that you have to kill before eating them. (Don't worry: It's all in 8-bit format, so kids don't see real violence.)

On a Minecraft farm, you can do things like shear sheep and collect wool. Thomas even created a farm that automatically breeds, hatches, collects, kills, and cooks chickens for eating later.

>> **Nutrition:** In Minecraft, you have to keep your character healthy. (Every default user is named Steve for boys, and Alex for girls.) Gathering nutritious foods best maintains your health. Try some beetroot soup. Or have an apple. Keeping your character's nutrition level stable helps the character last longer in the game.

>> **Art and architecture:** From full-tilt architecture to simply building fun designs and contraptions, you can express the artist in you in Minecraft. You can create dye from objects such as beets and flowers that you collect throughout the game. You can then use the dye to create panels to decorate your house, for example, or to color wool for other types of items in your house or dwelling place.

Players have created extravagant items such as ships and castles and even entire reproductions of various landmarks, such as the Eiffel Tower and the *Millennium Falcon* (from *Star Wars*). Entire cities have been reproduced in Minecraft. The sky is, quite literally, the limit.

» **Logic and math:** This is one of our favorite features because we're computer nerds. Joseph and Thomas (who wrote the previous edition of this book with me) are studying computer science and engineering in college, and my entire career has been in the tech world! Minecraft uses binary logic to implement contraptions from an electricity-like dust called *redstone dust.* You can use redstone to create logic-based devices that react in different ways based on power supplied to them. Even if your children don't realize it, creating redstone contraptions helps them learn binary logic, which is a primary element of programming and electronics that can be applied later in life. Check out Chapter 8 to see more about the topics your child can learn about with redstone.

» **Electronics:** When you're working with redstone, you're creating simple electronic and mechanical devices. Many of the devices work as transistors, capacitors, and even resistors to some extent, which are the basic building blocks of any electronic device or chip. If you can figure out how to compare the different redstone devices, you'll be able to help your child apply these contraptions to real life to build their own real-life robots and other fun, electronic devices.

TIP

We're big fans of LEGO Mindstorms. Using the concepts he learns about in Minecraft, Thomas builds real-life circuitry using LEGO blocks, a little programming, and some simple logic.

» **Computer programming:** Computer programming and electronics truly go hand in hand. Like electronics, computer programming uses logic to decide what happens in the computer program. Because the redstone circuits in Minecraft are virtual, each circuit is, in essence, a computer program.

In addition, you can do some fun things with actual computer programming if you want to let your kids experiment outside of Minecraft. For example, many players create their own mods of Minecraft to do fun things that are not natural to the game. Or you might let your kids set up their own Minecraft server and learn a little about systems administration in the process.

Knowing Where to Get Started with Minecraft

If you have kids or you work with kids (Minecraft is useful for teachers as a learning platform!), there's a good chance they're approaching you and asking you to buy Minecraft for them. Likely, they'll direct you to `http://minecraft.net` and ask you to buy them an account. This account is required if they want to play the PC version. If your kids are playing on a phone or on a game console like the Xbox or PlayStation, they don't need an account, but you still need to purchase the app to allow full gameplay.

In Chapter 2, we walk you through the entire process of setting up an account, including explaining the different types of Minecraft — whether you're on an Xbox or a PlayStation, a mobile device, a VR headset, or a PC or Mac. Go to Chapter 2 to find out more about getting started with Minecraft for the first time.

Keeping Your Kids Safe

As a single coparent of yes, seven children, I can relate to the constant, nagging feeling of wondering whether your kids are safe online. This feeling doesn't fade when your kids play Minecraft. Though I believe that Minecraft is a safer environment than lots of other games you can buy, I would at least follow a few principles to be sure that your children are staying out of trouble.

Knowing with whom your kids are playing

The biggest worry you should have as a parent of a child playing Minecraft, or perhaps any game or program, is not what they're playing but rather *whom* they are playing with. In the stand-alone game, players play alone, but if your children play on a server, they can be playing with *anyone,* anywhere around the world. And, in a game played mostly by children, predators are *undoubtedly* trying to take advantage of this situation.

Another concern about children playing games online is whom they're playing with in person. Knowing who is physically present at their friends' houses when they play can be critical information.

Here are a few tips to keep your kids safe as they play Minecraft with other people:

>> **Pay attention to whom they're chatting with.** Most interaction with players in Minecraft happens within the chat system. Your kids may even experience forms of cyberbullying (called *griefing*) that can trouble them, if you're not aware. You might want to look over your kids' shoulders every so often to understand what they're saying in chat and to ask them whom they're chatting with. You should know, and be comfortable with, every person your kids interact with in Minecraft.

>> **Establish a list of safe servers.** The easiest way to avoid griefing on Minecraft is to establish a safe list of servers that your kids can join. Find a server or two that you're comfortable with, and work with your children to ensure that they connect only with those servers.

>> **Set up your own server and establish rules on who can join.** This process may require a little more skill than you're willing to contribute, and the topic is well beyond the scope of this book. You can find many tutorials online, however, to show you how to set up your own Minecraft server. Doing so gives you the benefit of controlling what happens within the game and who is allowed to join. You can bar cursing and set gameplay rules, for example. My children play mostly on a server that our neighbors have set up, and the kids definitely know the rules that have been established.

>> **Don't play with strangers.** The old adage "Don't talk to strangers" applies to Minecraft as well. Though players have opportunities to meet new people in the game, these opportunities can be dangerous for minors if they don't know whom they're chatting with.

>> **Play with your kids.** The easiest way to keep your kids safe is to play the game with them. It's not only fun but also a wonderful opportunity to interact with your kids at their level, to learn the same concepts they're learning, and to provide teaching experiences in the process. In addition, you get to know the other players they interact with. Or, if the only person they interact with is you, that's okay too. We can't recommend this advice strongly enough. Who says that you have to interact with your kids only in real life? If they're still learning information that can improve their future, I say go for it!

Subscribing to Minecraft channels on YouTube

If your child is playing Minecraft, there's a pretty good chance that they not only play the game but also watch other people play it, *repeatedly*, on YouTube. We're extremely familiar with this phenomenon in our family: Minecraft is the new version of Saturday morning cartoons for our kids. They'd much rather watch Minecraft videos on YouTube than watch TV programs.

If the preceding paragraph describes your children, have no worries — your children are simply learning new ways to play the game. They're likely learning about new items they can create, and new ways to manipulate redstone and other blocks to build truly neat structures, which can likely apply to real-life knowledge.

Here are a few tips for protecting your children as they watch these videos:

>> **Watch videos only from channels they've subscribed to.** My kids can watch videos only on YouTube channels they subscribe to. I then have to approve each YouTube channel they're subscribed to. If we catch them watching a YouTube video on a channel they haven't subscribed to, or if they've subscribed to a channel we haven't approved, they're banned from watching YouTube videos.

   If a YouTube channel allows cursing or other objectionable material (you determine what's objectionable for your kids), it shows up in more than one video on their channel. So, if I see it on one video, I generally disapprove of the channel as a whole. This way, my kids are more likely to be watching videos only on channels that have safe content for kids.

>> **Watch a few of the videos your children watch.** Don't let your children randomly watch Minecraft videos. Objectionable, adult-oriented videos abound on YouTube, so be sure to establish a few guidelines to help your kids decide what to watch. Spend a little time watching a few of the videos your kids are watching. If you object, set some rules so that they don't watch the objectionable content again.

>> **Limit the amount of time your kids spend on YouTube.** Set some time limits to control how much time your kids spend on YouTube. If you need help, parental control software such as Norton Internet Security can allow you to set limits on how long your kids are online, and monitor the sites they have access to. Use that if you need to completely enforce time limits for your children. Or tally it on your own — you should always know how often your kids use the Internet.

>> **Place in a public area the computers your children use.** The best way to keep your kids safe is to put the computers they use in a public place in the home so that everyone can see what they're doing. This strategy also forces you to know more about what they're doing in the game (and other software). Our family also has a rule to prevent having mobile devices in our kids' rooms. Everything they do has to be in a public place so that we parents know what's going on.

>> **Talk to your kids.** By all means, maintain a continual dialogue with your kids to keep tabs on what they do in Minecraft. This strategy becomes even more important as they grow older and don't always play online at home. If they know they can talk to you about their experiences in the game, or on YouTube, or anywhere else on the Internet, they'll talk to you when they have problems or see things that make them uncomfortable.

TIP

You can subscribe to the official — and safe — YouTube channel for this book, managed by Joseph. (Figure 1-5 shows the *Minecraft For Dummies* YouTube channel.) You can subscribe to it at `http://youtube.com/minecraftdummiesbook`. At these sites, we share examples from this book — and much more.

FIGURE 1-5: The *Minecraft For Dummies* YouTube channel.

Teaching Proper Minecraft Etiquette

If you don't teach your kids good Minecraft etiquette, they may learn about it the hard way, by being banned from the server. Talk to them ahead of time, at their convenience, when they aren't playing the game. The following sections describe some best practices for interacting with other players.

Preventing server crashes

When playing on other people's servers, believe it or not, activities within the game can crash the server, causing undue stress for the person managing it. You should follow certain principles to avoid server overload. These are tips your kids ought to follow; otherwise, they may learn the hard way (by being banned from the server they're playing on).

>> **Mass explosions:** My son Joseph crashed a server he participates on by creating a contraption that produced unlimited dynamite (which shortly after explodes and destroys everything around it) in the game. So much dynamite was generated that it caused a massive explosion of dynamite, causing an infinite loop that eventually crashed the server. Our neighbor, the administrator of that server, asked Joseph not to create that contraption again.

>> **Infinite loops:** Anything that quickly produces an unlimited number of new items — explosions, spawn, or automated contraptions, for example — may cause undue stress on a server. Be careful not to do anything that is too complex for the server you're playing on to handle, to avoid being banned.

Recognizing that stealing is wrong

In real life, everyone knows that stealing is wrong. You may not go to jail, especially if you don't get caught, but stealing in Minecraft can get you banned from the server you play on. Sometimes it's fun to play pranks on other players in the game, but always remember that the server administrator can tell who is doing what in the game. You *will* get caught in the end.

In addition, vandalism and breaking items that others create are generally frowned on by most server managers. Treat other players' property with respect in Minecraft, and they'll treat yours with respect.

Asking permission

When in doubt, ask. If you're unsure whether a certain behavior is acceptable on a particular server, ask the server admin about it. Different servers have different rules and cultures, so what may be okay on one server may not be okay on another.

As a parent, see whether you can get to know some of the server admins on the servers your kids participate on. Get in the game and play with them. Chat with the admins or find out who they are. See whether you can find ways to get in contact with them and get to know them, or ask your kids about them. The more you know, the more you can help your children stay safe.

Chapter **2**

Scratching the Surface of Minecraft

You're ready to build, fight, create, craft, and brew. How do you begin? This chapter tells you how to register and begin your first game of Minecraft. As you undoubtedly have heard by now, Minecraft has taken the world by storm! These days, it's hard to be a gamer — or a gamer's parent — without hearing about, or at least coming across, the Minecraft brand. In fact, as of this writing, Minecraft is the most played game of all time.

Minecraft is a massive adventure you can play on your own, or with your friends. The adventure encourages exploration and, in effect, mining of the resources you need in order to build your world. As you play, you face monsters, zombies, and even dangerous animals that can hurt you along the way. You must keep yourself fed and nourished in order to stay strong. In so many ways, Minecraft mimics real life.

You have so much to learn about throughout this game: geology, architecture, farming, nutrition, and even electronics, engineering, and logic. Keep exploring — the more you learn, the cooler the items you can build.

Figuring Out Where to Play Minecraft: Console Round-Up

The game of Minecraft is playable across almost any device — console, computer, or phone. You'll find two current editions of Minecraft available: *Minecraft Bedrock Edition* and *Minecraft Java Edition*. Java Edition is available only for PCs, and *Bedrock Edition* is available on every device, including the PC. Older editions such as Legacy Console Edition or Pocket Edition may still be playable on certain devices, but they are considered obsolete and no longer receive content updates, whereas Minecraft Dungeons and *Minecraft: Story Mode* are separate spinoff games. The most professional of players will play on Java Edition, but Bedrock Edition is the most common and the easiest way to play.

TIP

Minecraft Bedrock Edition is the most common way to play the game, and it's the easiest way to buy the game. Any device other than a specific version on PC will run Bedrock Edition.

WARNING

Minecraft Bedrock Edition and *Minecraft Java Edition* aren't compatible — they have different servers and different player bases.

Purchasing and Installing Minecraft

To buy and install the game, log in to your Microsoft account at `http://minecraft.net`. Then follow these steps:

1. **Click the large Get Minecraft button on the home page.**

   The Minecraft Store page opens. This interface changes often, so the exact wording can also change as you read.

2. **Select the version of the game you want and the device you want to use to play the game.**

   As of this writing, the game cost $26.99 for PC, $29.99 for consoles, and $7.49 for mobile devices.

3. **Fill out the payment information, and then click the Proceed to Checkout button.**

4. **Follow the necessary steps to complete the purchase.**

If you bought *Minecraft Java Edition* and need to download it again, return to the Minecraft home page and follow the steps in the preceding list. When you see the Java Edition page, click the Download button.

The payment is immediately attributed to your account, so, if necessary, you can download the file again for free. The Minecraft home page also gives you the option to play from your browser — click the link under the Download Now button.

Playing the Game

After you install Minecraft, you're ready to start playing the game. To start, run the game and log in to your Microsoft account. You're finally ready to play!

Meeting the cast

After launching the game from the platform you have chosen, you will be greeted by the main menu. This menu holds all the key tools to starting your world, as shown in Figure 2-1.

FIGURE 2-1: The main menu in both editions.

This list describes what you can do after you click the buttons on the main menu in Java Edition:

>> **SinglePlayer:** Start or continue a basic game. This chapter covers the options for starting a game in SinglePlayer mode.

>> **MultiPlayer:** Join other players online. You can find more information about MultiPlayer mode in Chapter 12.

>> **Minercraft Realms/Realms Plus:** Buy a survival server that you and players you choose to invite can play on all at one time.

>> **Languages:** Change the language of the text in Minecraft. This tiny button, next to Options, is a speech bubble containing a globe.

>> **Options:** Manage game options such as sound, graphics, mouse controls, difficulty levels, and general settings.

>> **Quit Game:** Close the window, unless you're in In-Browser mode.

This list describes what you can do after you click the buttons on the main menu in Bedrock Edition:

>> **Play:** Start or continue a SinglePlayer game. Join a multi-player server, or view and join a friend's server.

>> **Settings:** Manage game settings such as sound, graphics, controls, and other general settings.

>> **Marketplace:** Visit the Minecraft store, where you can buy custom worlds, skins, and games and complete other activities.

>> **Dressing Room:** Change the "skin," which is another name for the appearance of your character, for your character's avatar.

In a SinglePlayer game, you (the player) are playing either as your own character or as Steve or Alex (the default characters), shown in Figure 2-2. In Minecraft, the ultimate objective is to defeat the ender dragon, a dragon that lives inside The End dimension. The focus of the game is to mine, craft, build, and explore your world and other worlds.

FIGURE 2-2: Steve and Alex.

Sorting out the gamemodes

Inside any world are three gamemodes you can choose from:

» **Survival:** In the original way the game is played, you play with the notion of being able to die; you receive no cheats or free items.

» **Creative:** You can fly, possess infinite items, and create whatever structures you want! This mode is best used for testing redstone, practicing building, or just plain ol' having fun.

» **Spectator:** Use this mode if you want to pass through blocks without collision, watch someone without them knowing you are there, or "spectate" your world without directly interacting with it. You're invisible in this gamemode except to other people in Spectator mode, you cannot break or interact with objects, and you can go through any block or player.

The For Dummies guide to Minecraft slang

Table 2-1 defines a few slang terms in Minecraft.

TIP

Minecraft is filled with specific mobs and terms. If you ever come across an unfamiliar mob or word, check out the Minecraft wiki at https://minecraft.fandom.com.

TABLE 2-1   Slang Terms, Defined

Term	What It Means
Mob	Any living creature — either a hostile mob or a docile mob — such as cow, horse, villager, or zombie. (This term is referenced often.) The term is short for *mobile entity*.
Respawn	When a player dies and reenters the world at their spawnpoint. Mobs do not naturally respawn.
Spawn	When a mob appears out of seemingly thin air in the world.
Spawnpoint	The location where a mob or the player spawns. The player's spawnpoint can be moved using a bed, command, or respawn anchor (see Chapter 12).
The Overworld	One of three dimensions (see Figure 2-3) in Minecraft. The Overworld is where you spend most of your time in Minecraft and where you initially spawn, and it's how you move between the other two dimensions.
The Nether	The second dimension in the game, a hell-like dimension covered in lava and fire. The Nether is home to many structures with unique mobs, and it's where you gather the necessary items to go to The End.
The End	The third, and final, dimension in the game. The End — which is the home of Minecraft's final boss, the ender dragon — consists of large islands (made of a tan brick called end stone) that float in a dark, endless void.
Entity	Any *active* object in the game — that is, one that isn't stationary, such as an item dropped on the floor, a mob, or an item frame.

FIGURE 2-3: The Overworld, the Nether, and The End.

Understanding basic controls

The world of Minecraft (you can see an example in Figure 2-4) is made of cubic *blocks,* or materials such as dirt or stone, that you can break down and rebuild into houses or craft into useful items. A block made of a material such as sand is referred to as a *sand block.* Because the side length of every block measures 1 meter, most distances are measured in blocks as well: If you read about an object that's located "3 blocks up," for example, it's the distance from the ground to the top of a stack of 3 blocks.

FIGURE 2-4: The look and feel of Minecraft.

In addition to building and crafting, you have to defend against enemy mobs and eventually face them head-on. As the game progresses, your goal becomes less about surviving and more about building structures, gathering resources, and facing challenges to gain access to more blocks and items.

To survive, you need to know how to move around, attack enemies, and manipulate the blocks that comprise the world. Get used to operating the controls, and become comfortable moving around.

The hostile and friendly mobs in the Overworld

During the first part of the game, you encounter a multitude of mobs — some friendly and others not so much. Knowing which ones can be approached is important in order to survive!

Passive mobs (as described in Table 2-2) won't attack you — no matter what. These mobs are always safe to be around. *Neutral* mobs can attack you when provoked in one way or another. *Hostile* mobs attack you unprovoked and are dangerous at all times.

REMEMBER

Neutral mobs (as shown in Table 2-3) can be both passive and hostile but are hostile only under specific conditions.

TABLE 2-2 **Passive Mobs**

Axolotl	Bat	Cat/ocelot
Chicken	Cod/Salmon	Cow/mooshroom
Fox	Frog	Squid/glow squid
Horse/donkey/mule	Parrot	Pig
Pufferfish	Rabbit	Sheep
Snow Golem	Tadpole	Tropical Fish
Turtle	Villager	Wandering Trader

TIP

Stay away from most hostile mobs (as shown in Table 2-4) at the beginning of the game. With no armor, and with most weapons unavailable, it's a bad idea to try to fight multiple mobs near the beginning.

TABLE 2-3 Neutral Mobs

Mob	Becomes Hostile When You Do This
Bee	Attack the bee, destroy the hive, or harvest the honey.
Spider/cave spider	Attack the spider or move too close while it's nighttime or very dark.
Dolphin	Attack the dolphin. And then it and the rest of its pod attack *you*.
Enderman	Attack (or even look directly at) the enderman.
Goat	Stand still near a goat for sometime between 30-300 seconds, and then it rams you.
Iron golem	Attack the iron golem or a villager near the iron golem.
Llama/trader llama	Attack the llama. In the case of a trader llama, it attacks you if you attack its wandering trade.
Panda	Attack the panda. If it's an aggressive variant, it attacks you.
Polar bear	Attack a polar bear or a cub and then all adult polar bears nearby become hostile.
Wolf	Attack a wolf and then the entire pack starts attacking you.

Discovering Tools

Tools are the basis of the game, and you can't make much progress without using them. Tools are used to collect and mine blocks faster than by hand.

TABLE 2-4 **Hostile Mobs**

Creeper	Drowned	Elder Guardian/guardian
Endermite	Evoker/vindicator	Husk/Zombie
Phantom	Pillager	Ravager
Silverfish	Skeleton	Slime
Stray	Vindicator	Witch

TIP

All tools have a durability. A tool can break only a certain number of blocks, or complete a specific task, before it breaks. A wooden pickaxe has a durability of 59, which means it can break 59 blocks before the tool breaks.

REMEMBER

What the tool is made of determines how fast it breaks a block, how much durability it has, and which blocks it can mine.

The materials used to make tools (which can all be seen in Figure 2-5) are described in this list, in increasing order of effectiveness:

- **Wood:** The lowest of the lot. It's mined slowly and is quite weak, and it has the second lowest durability. This tool is used to acquire cobblestone to make stone tools.

- **Stone:** Useful only when the game begins. It is mined faster than wood, it has slightly higher durability than wood, and it can be used to mine iron ore.

- **Iron:** The middle ground where tools are concerned. Iron has good durability and good mining speed, and, overall, it's used the most. It's used to obtain diamonds, gold, and other resources.

- **Gold:** The ultimate trade-off. Gold has the fastest mining speed of all tools, but has the lowest durability. Gold can mine anything that iron can.

- **Diamond:** The strongest tool that can be found in the Overworld. Diamond has a high durability and a fast mining speed, and it's all-around excellent.

- **Netherite:** Can be obtained only in the Nether and is the best of the best. With the highest durability and fastest mining speed, it's used to create the best set of tools in the game.

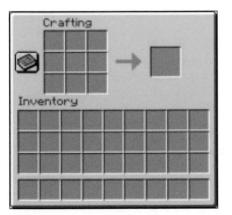

FIGURE 2-5: What the various materials look like.

Netherite tools, despite being the hardest to obtain, are still slower at mining than gold.

REMEMBER

The different types of tools are used for different purposes. A pickaxe specializes in mining stone, ores, and other blocks that are seen as more earthy.

The axe is used for faster mining of any wooden blocks. Most wood blocks can be mined by hand and still be collected, but an axe mines them faster.

A hoe is used for tilling dirt in order to sow seeds to grow plants. See Chapter 7 to learn more about farms.

A shovel is used to mine earthier and softer materials, like dirt or sand. Like the axe, most of these materials can be mined by hand, but are faster to mine with a shovel.

The sword is used to attack mobs. It has a faster attack speed than the rest of the tools.

TIP

Despite the sword's use as a tool for attacking, you can use an axe to attack as well. Axes do more damage than the sword, but have a much slower attack speed.

Interacting with Various Blocks

Minecraft is filled with placeable blocks. Every block has a use, in one way or another. Most blocks tend to be used only for decorative purposes, but some have additional behaviors or qualities you can make use of, such as being affected by gravity (sand), having a slippery surface (ice), or having a high blast resistance (obsidian).

The most useful blocks are *interactable,* which means that whenever you place the block, you can use it in some way. Interacting with these blocks opens a different window for you to use.

Other blocks that can be interacted with have more specific functions without using a menu. A campfire, for example, can have uncooked food placed on it in order to cook it. See Chapter 4 for more details about food.

Chapter **3**

Let's Go! Playing the Game and Surviving the First Night

A s the game opens, you have a few options to choose from. (Refer to Chapter 2 for a description of each of the buttons in both Java Edition and Bedrock Edition.) In this chapter, we focus on the Play tab and on creating a SinglePlayer world.

To start a brand-new world, choose from these three options:

» **Play (or SinglePlayer for JE):** Press Play and you're greeted by a screen where you can visit personal worlds, see friends online, and find MultiPlayer servers to play on.

» **Create New — Create New World:** From this menu, you can choose the world's name, gamemode, difficulty, and other world settings. In this chapter, we focus on the Survival gamemode.

» **Create:** After naming your world, press the Create button, and your world begins to load. In Bedrock Edition, you may be greeted by a message about staying safe online. Go ahead and accept the terms. Chapter 13 talks more about staying safe in Minecraft.

Viewing the World Around You

When you start a game, the loading screen describes how much of the world has been created. The world is automatically generated and is infinite. The way it generates is based on a magical number that you probably don't need to worry about now, called a *seed*.

You can input custom seeds that you find online, or simply input random ones. You can choose from many easy ways.

WARNING

Seeds between the Bedrock Edition and Java Edition are not the same. If you found a seed in a Bedrock World, you cannot use it for a Java World.

Operating the Basic Minecraft Controls

Minecraft is a tricky game on the surface level, and it's important to get used to the controls to easily maneuver through your world. Getting used to the controls makes all the difference in whether you die from being killed by hostile mobs, making a bad jump, or simply walking off a cliff. Table 3-1 introduces you to the basic movement and action options.

TIP

If you have a problem finding your key binds to perform these controls, go to the game settings and choose Keyboard and Mouse or Controller to view the key binds. In Java Edition, choose Options→Controls→Key Binds.

TIP

When sneaking, it's impossible to move off the edge of a block, which is useful for looking across ravines, placing blocks to create a bridge, and generally staying safe.

WARNING

Don't jump while you're on an edge, because you will die!

When first entering a world, move around a little to get used to the controls and make sure you know which buttons are set to which action. This way, whenever you start that first night, you won't stress about figuring out which button does what when encountering all those scary mobs. In Figure 3-1, you can see the world we first spawned in.

TABLE 3-1 **Basic Actions**

Action	Description
Walk	Use your analog stick or hold the button to move in the direction you are holding — it's as plain and simple as walking.
Sprint	Double-tap the Walk button or quickly jolt your analog stick forward twice. On the PC, you can also set a button to hold sprint for you. The default is the left control.
Break/attack	Both terms should be under the same button. *Break* means that you break a block and hold down the button on a block to do it. On the other hand, you tap the button to *attack* a mob.
Access Inventory	This action is essential to the game, and knowing it as second nature is crucial. Accessing your inventory is how you manage items, craft basic items, and view the items you have.
Interact/ place blocks	Usually, this action is bound to a single button. To interact with an object, you press the button while looking at the block. To place a block, look at where you want to place it and then press the button to place it. To place a block next to an interactable object, hold sneak while you place the block.
Sneak	This action is usually bound to a single button, which allows you to slowly move. It reduces the sounds you make, and it doesn't show your name to other players.
Drop	Use this button to drop an item you're holding, or to drop one from your inventory.

FIGURE 3-1: Where we first spawned in the world.

Watching the Heads-Up Display (HUD)

The little arrangement at the bottom of the screen is known as the Heads-Up Display, or HUD. To show the important details of your character, the HUD features the five sections described in the following list, as shown in Figure 3-2.

>> **Health bar:** These ten hearts monitor the health of your avatar. As your avatar incurs damage, the hearts disappear. After all ten hearts are depleted, your avatar dies and reappears at its *spawnpoint,* a position that can be changed by sleeping in a bed.

Your avatar can take damage by falling from ledges 4 blocks tall, colliding with harmful blocks or entities, or succumbing to other dangers, such as drowning. When you equip yourself with armor (see Chapter 10), the armor bar appears over the health bar, indicating the protective value of your armor.

>> **Hunger bar:** This bar represents the food supply. The emptier the bar, the hungrier you are. Hunger is an important concept to understand, so we cover it in Chapter 4.

>> **Experience:** The green experience bar fills up when you collect *experience orbs,* which appear naturally whenever you defeat monsters, smelt items in a furnace, breed animals, or mine any ore except iron or gold. When the bar is full, a number appears or increases over it, indicating your experience level. You can spend levels with anvils or enchantment tables (detailed in Chapter 10), but you will lose them if you die.

>> **Hot bar:** These nine squares, at the base of the HUD, contain items you've collected, and they're the only squares in the inventory that you can access without opening the inventory. You can use the numbers keys 1–9 or the scroll wheel on a computer or the left and right bumpers on a game controller to select items or blocks and then you can use that item. If you're using a sword or a tool for breaking blocks faster (such as an axe), the item automatically functions when you're breaking a block while operating your character, after selecting the item on the hotbar.

>> **Breath:** When your avatar's head goes underwater, ten bubbles appear just above the hunger bar and begin to pop, one by one. They signify how long you can hold your breath. If all the bubbles disappear and you're still underwater, the health bar begins to deplete.

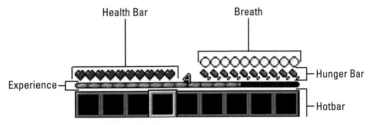

FIGURE 3-2: The Heads-Up Display.

Carefully monitor the health bar and hunger bar, and organize the inventory slots for organization. Developing this habit also tends to allow you to not die as often.

REMEMBER

Preparing for Your First Night

The first night is the hardest night of the Minecraft adventure. Preparing for the first night is *crucial.* The reason the night is scary is that hostile mobs start to spawn and spiders convert from being passive to hostile during the night. Minecraft is not for arachnophobes. Don't worry, though: Spiders are just as pixelated and kid-friendly as the rest of Minecraft.)

Minecraft's full day–night cycle is 20 minutes. When you first spawn in a world, you have 12 minutes until night falls and monsters start to spawn outside. Monsters only spawn for the remaining 8 minutes, which means that managing your time is vital to surviving your first night. See Table 3-2 for a description of what your first day should look like.

TIP

Harvesting trees

The first task you should complete when your world loads is to locate a tree and punch it — one of the main, and most popular, elements in Minecraft. To punch a tree simply means to break it with your bare hands (your selected item in your hotbar being empty). The overworld has six different types of trees, each in various sizes. (You can find more details about trees in Chapter 5.)

TABLE 3-2 Schedule for Surviving the First Night

Time	Task
Minutes 1–4	Find trees and start harvesting.
Minutes 5–7	Build a crafting table and tools.
Minutes 8–10	Build or find a shelter.
Minutes 11–12	Finalize any last-minute preparations, build weapons, and complete any other optional activities.

To start, chop down a couple of trees, which are made of wood blocks and leaf blocks. To break a block from the tree, follow these steps:

1. **Walk up to a tree.**

   See Chapter 1 for a rundown of the basic controls for moving in Minecraft.

2. **Position the crosshair over a wood block in the tree.**

3. **Hold the breaking/attacking button to start punching the block in Step 2 until the block breaks.**

4. **Collect the wood log that appears.**

   The log should come directly to you, but if you're too far away, just walk up to the log to collect it. The resource is added to the inventory at the bottom of the screen.

TIP

Leaves can be useful at this point in the game. After destroying the wood on a tree, the leaves will naturally start decaying. When they break naturally or by the player, they can drop sticks and apples! See below for using sticks to make tools, and Chapter 4 to learn more about food.

When you open the inventory, you can see a small 2x2 grid with an arrow pointing toward a single slot, labeled as crafting. To make wooden planks, simply place your chopped-up wood into the crafting grid in the inventory, and pull out the wooden planks that emerge from the single output slot. Each piece of wood should produce four planks.

Wood is a block that is used throughout the whole game, so gather a decent amount of wood at the beginning, approximately 16 to 32 wood logs. This supply will last you for a good few days before you need to chop down more trees.

Building a crafting table and shelter

The next steps in surviving your first night is to learn how to craft with a crafting table and building a shelter. Crafting will be used throughout the entire game and will be very helpful the first night.

Crafting the crafting table

Your avatar's crafting grid is a 2x2 square (refer to Figure 3-6); however, many items you need in order to survive require a 3x3 grid to craft. To unlock this larger grid, you build a crafting table. Follow these steps to build a crafting table, or *workbench*:

1. **Open the inventory.**

2. **Select the square containing the planks, and then place a plank on each square in the crafting grid to distribute four planks into the squares.**

   A crafting table appears in the right box.

3. **Select the crafting table and place it in one of the slots on the hotbar so that you can access it and place the crafting table on the ground.**

   You can access items outside the inventory screen only if they're on the bottom row. This row is always displayed at the bottom of the game screen.

4. **Leave the inventory.**

5. **Select the crafting table on the hotbar to have it show in your hand.**

   A thick, white outline appears around the crafting table.

   In Java Edition, you can use either the number keys or the scroll wheel to select items from the bottom row of the inventory. Place the most useful items in the slots you can quickly access.

6. **Place the crafting table on a nearby surface to access it.**

The crafting table is one of, if not the most, important block in Minecraft. Place it down and open it. The crafting table should look like the one in your inventory but in a 3x3 (rather than 2x2) shape.

When crafting, you see a little Book icon off to the left that you can select to help you make necessary items if you don't know the crafting recipe to create an item. Even if you have only some of the items needed for the recipe, the recipe shows up in the book and creates a template in the crafting menu of what you need. Figure 3-3 shows off what the Help Crafting menu looks like.

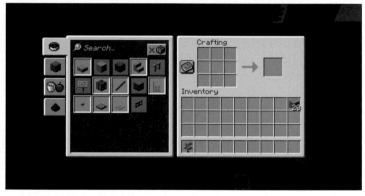

FIGURE 3-3: Using the Help Crafting menu.

Building or finding shelter

To survive your first night, we highly recommend that you either build a shelter or look for shelter. Shelters can range from a simple hut made from dirt to an elegant cave to hide from the monsters on the surface. If you plan to build your own structure, don't spend too much time on it at first. Keep it simple. We suggest digging into the side of a mountain, or have a house that projects from the side of a hill, because that is one less wall needed to be built and you have the later opportunity to make a cool base from the side of a mountain.

As you gain experience, you can invent your own architectural strategies. To build a basic shelter for now, follow these steps:

1. **Find a good building spot.**

Flat spots are the easiest to build on, but you can find any spot that you think is feasible for a house to fit. Remember that you can break and replace dirt, sand, and other blocks to flatten a rough area.

2. **Select a block from the inventory, and then place it on a nearby surface. Place several blocks in a comfortably sized outline for your base of operations, as shown in Figure 3-4.**

FIGURE 3-4: Starting your base.

Usually, the frame is a rectangle made of wooden planks, but you can collect blocks such as dirt and use them for building in a pinch. You also need a door, so you can leave one block out of the rectangle to make room for it. You can also build the rectangle around the crafting table so that you can work from inside your home.

3. **Place a second layer of blocks on top of the first layer.**

A structure that's two blocks tall is sufficient to keep most monsters at bay.

If you prefer to build or dig out a hole in the side of a hill or mountain, make sure you have a wooden pickaxe first, because you can't mine stone fast or collect it without one. Later in this chapter, we explain how to find a pickaxe. Once you have a pickaxe, try out these steps:

1. **Find a hill taller than your player.**

You need to have room in your dugout base, and you can't if the ceiling is too close to the surface.

2. **Mine a small cutout, to get in and out of your base, that your player will fit into before digging out.**

   This cutout is where you place the door to keep out mobs. You don't want the door to be left open for any mob to enter.

3. **Open enough space for you to work.**

   You don't need a ton of room to work — just enough for a crafting table, maybe a bed, and then any other blocks you want to place later. A dugout base we made is shown in Figure 3-5.

FIGURE 3-5: The dugout base we made on Day 1.

TIP

If you encounter a lot of stone while mining out your dugout shelter, craft a stone pickaxe (highly recommended) to mine much faster. This item is also great for mining the cobblestone and coal described in the "Completing Optional Day 1 Activities" section.

Next, craft a door so that you have a simple way to enter and exit the shelter. To build a door, use the crafting table and follow these steps:

1. **Open the crafting table menu.**

2. **Arrange six wooden planks in two adjacent columns of the crafting grid.**

   This arrangement is the recipe for a door.

3. **Move the door to the bottom row of the inventory.**

4. **Place the door in the wall of the shelter by placing the door on the ground wherever you want it.**

   You may have to break open part of the shelter wall to fit the door.

5. **Interact with the door to open (and close) it.**

REMEMBER

When you place a door in front of you, it's positioned to open away from you when you right-click on the door. Usually, a door is placed from the outside of a building so that it opens toward the inside.

TIP

To place a block beneath you, jump into the air while placing a block and looking straight down. This popular method for building and scaffolding is referred to as *pillar jumping*. If you repeat this strategy, you can effectively rise upward on a pillar of blocks, which is useful for building taller structures.

That's it — generally, a basic shelter can ensure your safety for the night.

If you plan to search for shelter and you see a village nearby, go to the village. A village is a helpful way to spend your first day and night: It's well-lit, it has food, and sometimes iron golems defend the village during the night. *Do not* hurt the iron golem or else it will kill you. Some villages have loot for you to take and use throughout your adventure! If you want to learn more about villages, flip to Chapter 9.

Making sticks and wooden tools

ALEX'S CORNER

Sticks and wooden tools set you on your way to obtaining many useful items. To create sticks, open the inventory or right-click the crafting table and put two vertically adjacent planks into the crafting grid. Four sticks are created for every two planks.

Sticks have no use on their own, but you can use them to craft a variety of other items. By arranging sticks and planks on a crafting table, you can create wooden tools. Tools are used for breaking blocks and fighting quickly and effectively, and although wooden tools break easily and work slowly, they provide a good start. Crafting recipes are shown in Figure 3-6.

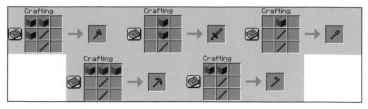

FIGURE 3-6: Crafting recipes for wooden tools.

Here's a rundown of wooden tools to create:

» **Wooden pickaxe:** You use this tool to mine stone-based blocks. (If you try to break stone by hand, it takes a long time and doesn't even drop an item.) Often, a pickaxe is the only wooden tool you need.

Any stone-based blocks you break while the pickaxe is selected break faster, so stash it in the bottom row of the inventory for quick access. Breaking stone blocks with a pickaxe produces cobblestone, which is used for stone-based products. (See Chapter 5 for information about the Stone Age).

» **Wooden axe:** Break wood-based blocks faster than by hand.

» **Wooden shovel:** Break granulated blocks faster, such as dirt, sand, and gravel.

» **Wooden hoe:** Till dirt or grass for farming wheat, carrots, potatoes, melons, and pumpkins. (See Chapter 7 for more on farming.)

» **Wooden sword:** Deal extra damage to enemies while this item is selected.

REMEMBER

When you use a tool, a green bar representing *durability* appears under the tool; the durability slowly depletes as you continue to use the tool. When the meter runs out, the tool breaks and you must craft a new one.

TIP

Only a pickaxe and sword are necessary for the first day. Other tools can be crafted after you discover stone.

Completing Optional Day 1 Activities

Your Day 1 activities should be, at the very least, to find a shelter, build a crafting table, and make a wooden sword and pickaxe. The following sections describe, if you have extra time, a few things you can do from there.

Building a full house

Building a basic shelter is already hard enough, but building a full-blown house is even harder! If this is what you want to live in for the first night, though, here are some helpful tips to help you on your way:

>> **Wood — lots and lots of wood:** Building materials at this point in the game are extremely limited, and wood or wooden planks are your only somewhat useful building block. Be sure to chop down lots of trees to allow yourself to start building more items.

>> **Focus on the outside before the inside:** You can work on the outside of the house during the day, but not at night. Build the outside during the day, for example. Then, for your first night, think about what you can do on the inside to make it a tidier house.

>> **Think small and then go big:** On your first night, you don't have much time. Consider starting by building a small house, and then think about how you can advance your house later.

Constructing a chest

When your avatar dies, you typically drop all items you've collected and you have to start over again or return to your death-sight (which could be dangerous since you died there) to pick up your items. Building a storage unit called a *chest* helps you store the items you've collected, even after you die and reenter the game. You can place a chest anywhere in your world and fill it with items you want to keep around in your world, even after you die.

To craft a chest, follow these steps:

1. **Interact with the crafting table to view the expanded crafting grid.**

Simply position the cursor crosshair over a placed crafting table and use the Interact button to view the crafting window.

2. **Confirm that you have at least eight wooden planks.**

    If you don't, chop down more trees, and then interact with the crafting table.

3. **Select the wooden planks to pick them up, and then place them in every square, except the center one, in the crafting grid.**

    This arrangement is for crafting a chest. The chest appears to the right of the arrow.

4. **Grab the chest, and then place it on the hotbar of the inventory.**

5. **Close the crafting menu the same way you open and close the inventory.**

6. **Place the chest somewhere nearby.**

If you interact with the storage chest, you can view an extra grid of squares that's almost as large as the inventory. Placing items into these slots stores them for safekeeping.

Always keep most of your valuables in storage when you're starting out. As you become more comfortable playing the game, you can carry more items with you, just in case.

WARNING

Do not place a block directly above a chest, or else it won't open.

TIP

Placing a second chest next to the first one creates an elongated chest, which stores twice as many stacks in the same place for more efficiency.

Mining cobblestone and coal

Cobblestone is a useful building and crafting material. Obtain this item by mining stone (a common, gray block) with a pickaxe. You can dig to find stone or look for a cave, mountain, or crag with a visible amount of stone.

This section also covers coal, the most common ore of the game, and how to obtain and use it. For more information about mining ores, see Chapter 8.

Table 3-3 explains how to obtain these items.

TABLE 3-3 **Basic Stone- and Coal-Based Items**

Tool	Name	How to Obtain It
	Stone tools	Crafted in the same way as wooden tools, except with cobblestone rather than wooden planks. Stone tools are faster and have twice the durability of wooden tools. Also, the stone pickaxe can mine lapis lazuli, iron ore, and copper (these materials are described in Chapter 8 and Chapter 10).
	Furnace	Crafted with eight cobblestone blocks. After you right-click the furnace, a new screen appears with two input slots and an output slot; place fuel in the bottom slot and an item in the top slot to cook the item. See Chapter 5 for more details about using the furnace.
	Coal	Used to craft torches and fuel furnaces. Coal can be found by mining coal ore, commonly found underground but occasionally aboveground. You can also cook wood blocks in a furnace to create charcoal, which has the same properties.
	Torch	Can be placed on a floor or a wall as a light source. These lights are always important because darkness provides a place for monsters to spawn — and you don't want them to appear in places where you need to go. Use a stick and a lump of coal to craft four torches.

TIP

If you make a shelter for your first night, having it lit up is impor- tant for ensuring sight and for preventing hostile mobs from spawning. Make a torch with one piece of coal and one stick. On the inventory's crafting menu, place the stick on either of the bot- tom squares and the coal directly above it. When you place down the torch, the room should light up. Don't worry: Though it's a torch, the flame won't dim.

Building a bed

If you're lucky enough to spawn somewhere that has sheep nearby, or a village, you're likely able to find or make a bed. Making a bed requires three wooden planks and three pieces of the same color of wool. When a sheep is killed, it always drops wool the color of the sheep. You can see how to craft a bed in Figure 3-7.

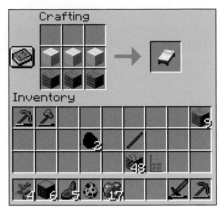

FIGURE 3-7: Crafting a bed.

TIP

Most houses in a village contain a bed — and if one house doesn't, you can always find another. For more specific information on villages and how beds in villages work, see Chapter 9.

Note that these two messages may appear onscreen and prevent you from sleeping:

>> **You can only sleep at night.** Wait until the sun sets a little more before trying again.

>> **You may not rest now, there are monsters nearby.** You must look for whatever creature is trying to kill you and destroy it before sleeping.

Continue working on the items in the earlier sections of this chapter until nighttime. That's when the fun begins.

Surviving the Night

Unless you set the difficulty level to Peaceful, you *will* face danger during the night. Table 3-4 describes the five types of enemies (and their variants) that appear during the night (look over the basic controls in Chapter 1, if you haven't already).

REMEMBER

Attacks inflict more damage when you're jumping. You can tell when you score a *jump attack* (jumping and hitting the enemy on your way down) by the wooden sparks emitting from the mob. Watch out, though: Jumping makes you hungry. (Read more about hunger in Chapter 4.)

TABLE 3-4 **Enemies and How to Defeat Them**

Enemy	Name	How to Defeat Them
	Creepers	Creepers are the most well-known enemies — these cute, green shrub-monsters walk toward you and hiss and then explode, harming you and destroying nearby blocks. Attack while sprinting (double-tap the W key) to knock back creepers before they explode. When you play in a higher difficulty mode, creepers can kill your avatar in a single shot.
	Endermen	Endermen might not appear on the first night, but sooner or later you'll see one. Don't antagonize these monsters — they can be challenging even for experienced players. See Chapter 2 to see when they will start attacking you. Endermen are 3 blocks tall, and you're only 2, so you can hide behind a tree that is 2 blocks tall and it can't reach you.
	Skeletons/Strays	Skeletons are downright tricky: They approach you tactically and fire arrows at you. Skeletons are impeccable archers, so hide behind blocks to avoid them. They shoot faster as you move closer, so sneaking up on them is your best bet.
	Spiders	Spiders have a relatively small amount of health, but they're fast, small, and jumpy, making them difficult to hit. They can also climb walls, so be prepared to defend your shelter.
	Zombies/Husks	Zombies are fairly easy to vanquish if you see them coming. They have more health than other enemies, but they move slowly. Don't let them stall you long enough for other monsters to notice you.

Switching from Peaceful mode to Easy mode to Normal mode

If you're playing in Peaceful mode, no harmful mobs can spawn — much less attack — and surviving the first night isn't the goal. Instead, your focus should be on advancing through other challenges. You can continue navigating the other challenges of Minecraft in the following chapters. However, if you're ready for a fight, you can switch the difficulty setting to Easy at any time by using the Pause menu.

If you select the default difficulty, Normal mode, you find that the game balances the elements of Minecraft — surviving, building, crafting, gathering resources, and farming, for example. The mobs are challenging, and it can be difficult to combat hunger (see Chapter 4). This chapter tells you how to survive the first night and continue through the game. However, younger players or those who don't want the distractions of mobs and hunger as they explore Minecraft can switch from a difficult mode to an easier one.

TIP

If you have small children or just don't like dying or exposing your kids of a certain age to death or killing and weapons in general, Peaceful mode is a safer way to introduce your children to Minecraft without pixelated violence and still reap most of the benefits!

TIP

Normal mode is a good choice for players who like a significant challenge from mobs while playing the other parts of Minecraft — such as building, farming, mining, excavating, and inventing.

REMEMBER

In Easy mode, you must protect yourself at night from mobs and worry about hunger (see Chapter 4). Easy mode provides a bit more of a challenge with only a small risk of losing early in the game. If you aren't against death or killing pixelated imaginary monsters, we suggest this mode over Peaceful mode. In the remainder of this chapter, we focus on giving you the necessary information to survive your first night in Easy mode.

Surviving the first night: Three strategies to light the way

The first night can be a doozy if you're not prepared! Knowing a few simple strategies can help you make it out alive and set the pace to stay alive (you hope) throughout the game.

Strategy 1: Implement the basic strategy

The first approach we suggest that you take to survive the night is basic, and it's one used quite frequently by players of Minecraft. Here's a summary of the basic strategy, outlined earlier in this chapter:

1. **Harvest trees by punching wood.**
2. **Build a crafting table.**

3. **Construct a shelter.**

4. **Craft wooden tools and a sword.**

TIP

If you're playing in Peaceful mode, it isn't necessary to build a shelter or sword. You can choose any optional activities or try your hand at building an effective house.

In the basic strategy, the night can get quite boring to just wait inside your shelter. Try building a mine inside your shelter while you wait. See Chapter 8 to find out more about how to start a mine.

Strategy 2: Use the safe strategy with popular optional activities

Though the first strategy we discuss prepares you for the night, it leaves a bit of risk and little protection. Our second strategy for surviving the night ensures that you've covered all the bases to make yourself completely safe. These steps, though they perhaps require a little more work to achieve, ensure a peaceful night of sleep, with little interruption from mobs on your first night.

To start the safe strategy, follow these steps:

Here are the steps:

1. **Harvest trees.** You can do so by punching wood.

2. **Create a crafting table and chest.** See the section "Building a crafting table and shelter," earlier in this chapter.

3. **Craft tools and weapons.** See the section "Completing Optional Day 1 Activities," earlier in this chapter.

4. **Find and kill sheep and craft a bed.** Just like in real life, in Minecraft sheep are one of the animals you can kill to obtain meat to feed yourself and wool to build beds and other necessities. Fortunately, the sheep in Minecraft are 8-bit pixel animals, and the killing is hardly violent. After you've killed some sheep, you'll want to craft a bed. See the section "Building a bed," earlier in this chapter, to see how, with the wool you've collected from the sheep.

5. **Create a simple shelter.** See the section "Building a crafting table and shelter," earlier in this chapter, to find out how.

6. **Trap animals other than sheep.** Using the remaining daylight, look for animals and trap them by digging a hole, trying to get at least two of each animal (see Chapter 7 for more information on animals). Trapping animals allows you to have food and energy when you need it, and when you have more than one animal, you can breed them together and create a farm (see Chapter 7 for more about this strategy)!

7. **Look for caves or dig a staircase mine.** You can do this by looking for caves or digging a staircase mine. (This step is necessary to build a furnace, as discussed in the section "Completing Optional Day 1 Activities" earlier in this chapter.)

Strategy 3: Plan an adventure strategy

The strategy we describe in this section is for more adventurous players, who are comfortable fighting a mob or two and who want to take much more risk on their first night:

1. **Harvest trees.**
2. **Create a crafting table, tools, and weapons.**
3. **Find and kill sheep and craft a bed.**
4. **Start traveling.** Start moving and look for anything — a cave, a village, or even a pyramid! Villages work well for starter homes, but you'll have to fight off the zombies.

REMEMBER

This strategy is targeted at exploring the Minecraft world nomad-style rather than creating a large house (or base) with connecting farms and mines. There's no single correct way to play Minecraft!

REMEMBER

If you have crafted a bed and sword, you don't need a shelter, because you can either fight off mobs or sleep the night away.

You can choose from plenty of other successful strategies using a combination of required and optional Day 1 activities. Many players like to experiment with different ideas and strategies every time they play, whereas others stick to a single method that proves effective.

When it's daytime again, the world becomes safer. The undead catch fire in sunlight, spiders no longer attack you, and endermen disappear as they teleport away from the harmful light; creepers are still harmful, but they eventually leave as well. If you're in any mode other than Peaceful mode, congratulations on surviving your first night! Now you can turn your attention to mastering the basic skills needed to survive hunger.

TIP

If you're truly in a dire situation, try burrowing into the ground and waiting. Make sure that no mobs can get into your hiding hole. The night lasts 8 minutes and 20 seconds. Use this time to strategize your next day, consume some snacks, or just take a short break from the game.

2

Getting a Handle on the Basic Skills

IN THIS PART . . .

Staying fed and finding food

Learning to mine basic blocks

Getting to know the main Minecraft biomes

Chapter **4**
Surviving Hunger

After surviving the first night, you need to find and eat food while you accomplish the next challenge in the game — implementing blocks, farming, or mining, for example. This chapter can help you understand how the food system works in Minecraft so that you can keep yourself well fed as you continue in the game.

Keeping Hunger at Bay

Hunger is a dangerous, long-term obstacle. Try to overcome it as efficiently as possible, which ultimately means gathering as many animals as possible in an area you control by farming. But you must eat while you create farms and overcome the obstacles presented, not to mention survive nightly mob attacks, in order to stay alive. As depicted by the hunger bar at the bottom of the screen, you grow hungry over time, and you require food in order to resolve the hunger.

REMEMBER

In Peaceful mode, the health bar doesn't deplete from your hunger, so you can continue to the next challenge without acquiring or eating food. However, when the hunger bar drops down to three bars or less, you cannot move quickly (by sprinting).

Eating food restores your character's health (as depicted by the hearts on the health bar) indirectly over time. After eating, if the hunger bar becomes full, you gain one full heart every second until your hunger drops by one point. Though your character never dies from hunger except in Hard mode, it makes you vulnerable to damage that can kill you, including relatively small damage such as touching a cactus, falling from a four-block height, or even facing attacks from neutral mobs.

TIP

If hunger is significantly limiting gameplay, you can switch to Peaceful mode or Easy mode while you start a farm (see Chapter 7).

Your symptoms of hunger depend on the difficulty level. Except in Peaceful mode, your character grows hungrier with every action you take: Sprinting or attacking is the easiest way to deplete hunger units, but jumping or absorbing damage also taxes your character.

REMEMBER

You cannot sprint if the hunger bar has three units or fewer.

The consequence of famine (as depicted by an empty hunger bar) depends on the difficulty level, as outlined in Table 4-1.

TABLE 4-1 The Effects of Famine on Your Character

Difficulty Level	What Happens to the Health Bar
Peaceful	Doesn't deplete
Easy	If it's more than half-full, slowly depletes until it's half full
Normal	Slowly depletes, but not to the point of death
Hardcore	Depletes until it's empty (find some food — quick!)

To refill the hunger bar, you need to acquire and eat food as described in the later section "Finding food."

When the hunger bar is depleted by one full point, you gain half a heart every 4 seconds until you're at full health, or until your hunger depletes by one-half more.

Finding food

If you're starting a new game, strive for the foods described near the top of Table 4-2, because they're the easiest to find and make. The table explains how to obtain several useful foods. (Chapter 4 has more information about the items themselves.)

TABLE 4-2 **Useful Foodstuffs**

Icon	Food	Description
	Raw porkchop or beef	Killing a pig or cow grants you from 1 to 3 units of this food. However, the food is more effective when cooked.
	Cooked porkchop or steak	Cook raw meat to obtain an item worth 4 units of food.
	Raw chicken	Avoid eating raw chicken unless you must. Every raw-chicken item you eat gives you a 30 percent chance of getting food poisoning, draining the hunger bar.
	Cooked chicken	It has the same effect as cooked porkchop or steak, but, at 3 units of food, is less powerful.
	Mushroom or beetroot stew	This item restores 3 units of food, and each inventory space holds only one bowl of stew.
	Bread	Bread isn't quite as satiating as meat, but after you obtain a wheat farm (as described in Chapter 7), you can craft a reliable food source, 2½ units in strength.
	Cookie	Cookies are crafted from wheat, but you also need cocoa beans. Cookies restore only 1 unit of food apiece, so they aren't quite restorative — though you can mass-produce them.
	Carrot	Carrots are found incidentally whenever you kill zombies or explore villages (as described in Chapter 9). A carrot provides 2 units of food.
	Potato	Potatoes are also found incidentally. Raw potatoes aren't useful, though they can be cooked into baked potatoes.
	Baked potato	Cook potatoes to get this item, worth 3 units of food.
	Melon slice	Despite the meager effect of a single slice, or 1 unit, this item can be mass-produced effectively.

(continued)

TABLE 4-2 *(continued)*

Icon	Food	Description
	Red apple	This fruit falls from destroyed trees and provides 2 units of food.
	Golden apple	Each golden apple yields 2 units of food. Crafted with gold, it boosts health and reduces hunger. It also yields regeneration, fire resistance, and resistance status effects. (See Chapter 11 for more info about these topics.)
	Raw cod	Raw fish can be obtained by fishing or killing fish in the water. Each raw fish is worth 2 units of food.
	Cooked cod	Cook fish to get this item, worth 6 units of food; it makes a good food source if you have time on your hands.
	Pumpkin pie	Collect eggs (littered by chickens), sugar (from lakeside reeds), and pumpkins to make a pie worth 4 units of food.
	Cake	Making a cake requires 3 buckets of milk, 2 lumps of sugar, 3 units of wheat, and 1 egg. Cake has to be placed on the ground before you can eat it; right-click it to restore 1 unit of food. Cake disappears after six uses.
	Rotten flesh	Eating rotten flesh — obtained from zombies — gives you an 80 percent chance of food poisoning.
	Sweet Berries	Found in the "lush cave" biome (see Chapter 8), it provides easy to get food while mining. Restores 2 hunger points.
	Raw salmon	Obtain this item from fishing or killing salmon; it's good for eating and for taming ocelots. Restore 2 hunger points.
	Cooked salmon	Simply cook salmon to restore 6 hunger points.
	Poison potato	Restores 2 hunger points but has a 60 percent chance of poisoning a character for 4 seconds; unlike a regular potato, it cannot be planted or baked.

Icon	Food	Description
	Raw mutton	Killing sheep drops 1 or 2 units of mutton, providing 2 hunger units when eaten raw.
	Cooked mutton	Mutton cooked offers 6 hunger points — more than chicken but less than pig or beef.
	Raw rabbit	When a rabbit (or bunny) is killed, it drops 0-1 units of raw food, which can be eaten for 3 hunger points (more than most other types of raw meat).
	Cooked rabbit	Rabbit cooked, it increases the hunger points to 5, just slightly less than cooked mutton.
	Rabbit stew	This complicated recipe involves a bowl, a carrot, a baked potato, a mushroom, and a cooked rabbit; but when crafted and then eaten, it restores an incredible 10 hunger points.
	Sweet berries	Gather the berries by interacting with a sweet berry bush, or break the bush. These can only be found in Taiga biomes (more info in Chapter 6). Each sweet berry restores 2 hunger points.

REMEMBER

On the hunger bar, each drumstick represents 2 food units.

Note that cooked meat provides two to three times more food points than raw but requires using a smoker or campfire or furnace (see Chapter 3) or killing the animal via fire, such as lava or flint and steel.

WARNING

Eating poisonous food can significantly impact the health bar and hunger bar. Except in Hard mode, you won't die directly from poison, though you're extremely vulnerable to any type of damage and your ability to complete activities decreases. Drinking milk negates the effects of poisonous food. However, obtaining milk isn't possible until you're further into the game, when you have the resources to craft a bucket.

Chapter **5**

Discovering Blocks and Items

You have survived your first night and now the game truly begins — you can now choose what to do with your world. This chapter guides you in identifying various blocks and tells you what they do and how you can use them. Your knowledge of blocks helps you choose what to do and where to explore in your world.

Starting in the Wooden Age

The Wooden Age is where you start the game in Minecraft. After the first night ends, you should have collected at least a wooden pickaxe and a wooden sword. You should also mine stone to create stone tools after the first night is complete. Stone tools are a massive upgrade from wood. (See Chapter 3 for the tools' crafting recipes.)

The overwhelming need for wood

Just because you have stone tools doesn't mean that you have no need for wood. Wood is almost a constant necessity in the game. Wooden planks are the most often used item for crafting recipes.

Because of the need for wood, you must make sure you have a consistent and easy way of collecting the wood. As you're playing, do you notice, after chopping down the wood in a tree, that the leaves break naturally? When this happens after a leaf breaks, the leaf has a chance to drop a sapling or an apple. You can also break the leaves with your hand or a hoe for faster mining and have the same chance for that leaf to drop an apple or a sapling.

REMEMBER

Saplings are the plants you need in Minecraft to grow trees. When you place a sapling in the Minecraft world, it takes at least 30 minutes to grow. Saplings don't grow without sufficient light and sufficient space. When a sapling has no room to grow, it remains a sapling. The space needed for a sapling to grow is determined by the size of the tree. The various tree sizes are shown in Figure 5-1.

FIGURE 5-1: Varioius sizes of trees found in Minecraft.

TIP

If you're waiting for a sapling to grow, you can use bonemeal to speed up the process. (To find out more about bonemeal, visit Chapter 7.)

There's a wood for that

Minecraft has seven types of trees in the Overworld, each with its own corresponding wood. Though each wood has its own planks, logs, doors, and trapdoors, every other recipe that requires wood can be crafted with all types of wood. Table 5-1 shows every type of wood and lists the biome where it's found. (See Chapter 6 for info about biomes.)

WARNING

Table 5-1 lists every type of wood that can be found in the Overworld. There are two types of wood that can be found in the Nether that you can learn more about in chapter 11.

TABLE 5-1 ## Wood Types

Wood	Biome
Oak	All Jungles, Dark Forest, Forest, Meadow, Plains, River, Savanna, Swamp, Wooded Badlands, Windswept Forest
Spruce	All Taigas, Snowy Plains, Windswept Forest, Grove
Birch	Birch Forest, Dark Forest, Forest, Meadow
Jungle	All Jungles
Acacia	Savanna
Dark oak	Dark Forest
Mangrove	Mangrove Swamp

TIP

When we make wooden structures and builds, our favorite wood to use is spruce — its attractive appearance makes for great-looking bases. The type of wood you use doesn't matter, but for creativity and building, having a variety is useful.

Pillaging and Plundering

After you have a good grasp of your world and you understand why you need wood, it's time to explore. The world contains many hidden features and neat-looking structures to find and explore. One of the easiest items to find in the beginning of a game is a village (see Chapter 9) or, if you're near an ocean, a shipwreck (see Figure 5-2).

FIGURE 5-2: A shipwreck in the ocean.

Knowing when to loot and when not to

Looting in Minecraft simply refers to taking resources from a chest that isn't yours. Chests that are naturally generated in the world are always a part of a structure or a building that was generated automatically by Minecraft for your world. (You can find a description of all the various structures and types of loot in Chapter 6.)

Looting, which is a helpful way to obtain beginning-to-midgame items and resources, can produce items ranging from an apple or bread to diamonds or iron; most land somewhere in between.

Here are some of the do's and don'ts to looting in Minecraft:

>> Do take items from villages and other structures in the Overworld that are easy to obtain.

>> Don't go looking in structures without proper equipment — find a safe way instead to reach the loot you want.

>> Do create an easy escape plan if you're looting in a more dangerous area.

>> Don't look inside structures without first being aware of the dangers and traps.

TIP

Looting eats up lots of inventory space, so keep a base or house nearby to drop off items you want to keep. Looting can also be quite dangerous, and dying far from home with all your valuables on hand is frustrating. Just as your mother might have said to you (if you're lucky) after you moved out of her house, feel free to visit home often.

Where to go, what to find

When you're searching for resources, knowing which items you need and which ones you can leave behind is always helpful. Table 5-2 shows you every useful item that can be found from looting.

Surviving the Stone Age

The Stone Age is where you start the mining process. To upgrade tools, armors, or other equipment, you must mine for it or find it while exploring. Mining is much more efficient for collecting specific resources and ores, whereas exploring and looting are good for finding items that are more useful. (If you want to find out more about mining, Chapter 8 is for you.)

The cheap and plentiful

The best and most useful part of the Stone Age is realizing how many items and blocks you can obtain. Dirt, cobblestone, coal, and iron are all plentiful resources and should be used accordingly.

TABLE 5-2 **Useful Items from Looting**

Name	Description
Diamond anything	In chests, you can occasionally find diamonds, diamond tools, or diamond armor.
Gold anything	Gold is an overall useful resource. You should have at least one piece of gold armor (see Chapter 11).
Iron anything	Iron — the great equalizer — is a middle-ground resource. It's used for a lot of crafting, mining, and defense and is useful in the beginning, up to midgame.
Golden apple/ enchanted golden apple	Although regular golden apples are craftable and relatively easy to make, *enchanted* golden apples can be found only in naturally generated chests. Be sure to grab one whenever you can. The enchanted golden apple is helpful if you're in a pinch and need health. (See Chapter 11 to find out more about this item.)
Music discs	Music discs are difficult to find, and chests are one of two ways to collect them. The discs can be played in jukeboxes, which we describe later in this chapter, in the section "Using Utility Blocks."
Horse armor	Iron, gold, and diamond horse armor can be found only in chests and can't be crafted, but leather horse armor can. It can't break, either, so unless you plan to have more than one horse, only a single armor is necessary.
Nametags	Nametags can be found only in chests. If you find one, snag it. (See Chapter 10, and its discussion of anvils, to learn more about nametags.)
Enchanted book	Enchanted books are useful and can be applied to specific equipment.
Chainmail armor	Chainmail armor (which looks good on a player) can be found in chests, dropped by mobs that spawn while wearing it, or bought from armor villagers (see chapters 7 and 9 for about villages). It's slightly better than gold armor (but has a much higher durability) and slightly less than iron.
Potions	Potions are good to use in a pinch or whenever you want to power up, gain health, or breathe underwater, for example. (Potions are described in depth in Chapter 10.)
Saddle	A saddle, which is another uncraftable item, can be found in chests or bought from a leatherworker. Saddles are used to ride specific mobs and control them.

Name	Description
Crossbow	A crossbow can be crafted or found by killing pillager mobs. Crossbows can be enchanted and are good weapons to have if you don't have a long-range weapon.
Enderpearl	Enderpearls are needed for reaching The End and are also useful items on their own. You can throw an enderpearl by clicking the Interact button. When the enderpearl lands, it teleports you to wherever it landed.
Food	When you're on an adventure, you don't want to run out of food and have to go looking for plants or animals. So it's always a good idea to grab some extra food if you see it — especially golden carrots and cake.

TIP

Don't let cobblestone fool you by its appearance — it may look relatively ugly in its current state, but when you put a piece of cobblestone in a furnace and smelt it, stone is made.

Stone is useful when used with a stonecutter to make prettier blocks, but stone is also good for creating stone bricks, using your inventory's Crafting grid. One time, after mining in a world, we took all the cobblestone and turned it into stone and stone brick so that we could build a glorious castle!

The necessities

During the Stone Age period of the game, we like to simply gather resources and items to make ourselves more powerful or to make our home or base more comfortable. Stone is also the foundation of lots of crafting recipes in the game.

The most notable recipes are described in this list:

>> **Brewing stand:** This useful utility block is how potions are made. The stand is made with three cobblestone blocks and one blaze rod. Blaze rods are obtained from the Nether, as described in Chapter 11. (Potions and brewing are found in Chapter 10.)

>> **Lever:** Levers are helpful on–off devices that are made with one cobblestone block and one stick. They can be used for doors and trapdoors, and they're fun for decorations.

>> **Furnace:** The most important item on this list, furnaces are made with eight cobblestone blocks. Furnaces are how you smelt ore and other materials. We explain them in detail later in this chapter, in the section "Smelting and cooking."

The path to iron

The path to iron from stone is a simple one. You must mine iron ore to collect raw iron and smelt it in a furnace to create iron ingots. The Iron Age is where you'll start having trouble, which we explain later in this chapter. It's where the middle of the game starts and getting there should be a high priority near the beginning of the game.

After acquiring stone tools and learning a little more about the game, you can start the beginning of your mining career. Simply dig a staircase shape into the ground or find a cave to mine in.

WARNING

Do not dig straight down. Doing so can lead to sudden falls, which will certainly lead to death. Digging straight down also does not allow you an easy retreat if you need to exit a cave.

In a cave or just by happenstance, you will come across iron ore, as shown in Figure 5-3. You can use a stone pickaxe to mine the iron ore and get raw iron, also shown in the figure.

FIGURE 5-3: Raw iron and iron ore.

After acquiring as much raw iron as you need, you can take it back to your furnace, use coal or wood as fuel, and smelt it into iron ore.

Advancing to the Iron Age

The Iron Age is where we spend a lot of time in the game. It's the age of the game where you can start to collect almost every resource and gain enough of a power boost to feel more comfortable exploring and fighting mobs.

In the Iron Age, you should

>> **Mine:** Collect all necessary ores and upgrade to diamonds. This is a big part of the Iron Age. Mining progresses you further into the game and gives you more items to use.

>> **Suit up:** You make your first handcrafted armor out of iron, allowing you to absorb more damage so that you can survive longer.

>> **Strap up:** Learn about the different types of weapons, such as how to craft them and how best to use them. Get used to using the weapons on mobs and other creatures.

REMEMBER

Crafting iron tools is performed the same way as with wood or stone tools except that — rather than wooden planks and cobblestone — you use iron ingots.

When we first go mining for iron, we normally collect 34 raw iron blocks before leaving, an amount that is enough to craft all tools (except a hoe), a full set of iron armor, and a shield. Table 5-3 shows crafting recipes for the armor.

TABLE 5-3 How to Craft Armor

Armor Piece	Crafting Recipe
Helmet	
Chestplate	
Leggings	
Boots	

To put your armor on, open your inventory and move an armor piece to the left of the player. The armor pieces can be placed from top to bottom: helmet, chestplate, leggings, boots.

Making and mastering weapons

Weapons in Minecraft boil down into two groups: melee weapons and ranged weapons. *Melee* weapons inflict more damage when you directly hit the mob character with the Attack button. *Ranged* weapons can be used to attack from a distance.

Weapons and their crafting recipes are listed in Table 5-4.

TABLE 5-4 **How to Craft Weapons**

Sword	
Axe	
Bow	
Crossbow	
Trident	The only way to obtain a trident, which isn't craftable, is to kill the drowned mob that's holding it. And then there's only an 8.5 percent chance that the mob will drop the trident.

TIP

Tridents are used as both a melee weapon and a ranged weapon by throwing them. Tridents, which are difficult to obtain, deal the same amount of damage as a diamond axe but have a slower cooldown time.

REMEMBER

Axes deal more damage than their sword counterparts, but they use more durability and have a much slower cooldown time. Because of this, swords have a higher damage-per-second rate. You also deal critical hits by jumping before you hit a mob character with a melee weapon.

Stringing the bow

Bows and crossbows are helpful at long range. On a bow, you can shoot arrows by holding down the Interact button with a bow selected and arrows in your inventory. Release the button after your character has stopped pulling back on the bow to shoot the arrow.

Crossbows work the same way, but you can ready one by reloading it in the same way as a regular bow — when you release the button, however, it doesn't shoot. Instead, you must press the button again to shoot it. After stringing a crossbow, you can have it ready to shoot by just leaving it in the stringed position.

Crossbows inflict more damage than bows but take longer to shoot.

TIP

Because you can leave crossbows ready to shoot, you can also leave multiple crossbows on the hotbar and ready to shoot. Then, whenever you're faced with an enemy mob, you can shoot each crossbow on the hotbar, one after another. This trick deals a quick burst of damage to any enemy.

Strapping the shield

The shield is a unique addition to the game — it allows you to block hits and damage inflicted by mobs. As we write this chapter, there's only one way to craft a shield, so there are no better or worse shields.

After crafting a shield, you place it in your off-hand, by placing it in the open spot that displays a shield logo to the right of your player in the inventory. With an equipped shield, you can hold the Interact button with a sword or tool in hand, or by having the cross-hair positioned toward nothing in order to block with the newly acquired shield. Holding a shield forces you to move at sneak speed.

While you're blocking with a shield, arrows and standard attacks from mobs inflict no damage on you, but they do reduce the shield's durability. Using a shield allows you to block a creeper from exploding next to you, a skeleton from shooting you, a zombie from hitting you, and much more.

REMEMBER

If you're playing with another player and you end up fighting that player, an axe striking a shield disables the shield for 5 seconds. During this time, you cannot block any other item with that shield.

Using Utility Blocks

A *utility block* is any kind of block that shows a menu after interacting with the block. Utility blocks are used for crafting, smelting, enchanting, and making potions, for example. The block is an essential part of both upgrading and decorating tools, blocks, and other items.

Smelting and cooking

Quite a variety of utility blocks specialize in either smelting an item (extracting ingots from ores) or cooking items like food. Table 5-5 shows off all the utility blocks that can do either task.

TABLE 5-5 Smelters and Cookers

Name of Block	Crafting Recipe	What It Does
Furnace		The furnace is the foundation of smelting and cooking. It can smelt or cook at a base rate. Simply put fuel in the bottom block and the item to be heated in the top block.
Blast furnace		This upgraded furnace, which specializes in smelting, works twice as fast as a normal furnace with ores, raw materials, and armor. It cannot be used for any other purpose.
Smoker		A smoker is used to cook food twice as fast as with a furnace. It can only cook food, though.
Campfire		A campfire has no menu, but when you interact with it with food in your hand, it places the food near the fire. And when the food is cooked, it automatically pops out of the campfire.

TIP

Furnaces and blast furnaces not only smelts ores and raw materials, but they can also melt gold, iron, and chainmail tools and armor. Rather than toss all that old armor, just place it in a blast furnace with some fuel and you can get back some of your ingots.

Jukebox and note block

The jukebox and note block are both used for creating music. After you place a jukebox, you can insert a music disc you found by exploring. Each music disc's name corresponds to the song that the disc plays when it's in the jukebox. The game now has 14 music discs — try to collect them all.

When you interact with a note block, it produces a sound based on whichever block it appears under. Noteblocks have a vast range of sounds, including melodic instruments like piano, guitar, xylophone, and much more but also percussive instruments like snare drum, cow bell, and bass drum.

Stonecutter and loom

The *stonecutter,* originally available for *Minecraft Pocket Edition* (only on mobile devices), is a helpful block for easily crafting useful decorative and fancy blocks. This list includes stairs, slabs, walls, and some exclusive novelties. To craft a stonecutter, you need three stone and one iron ingot. After interacting with the stonecutter, place the block of choice in the "input" square and select the preferred output of the block.

The *loom* is a block used to customize banners. A banner is a useful way to display a logo, an emblem, or other fun patterns. To craft a loom, you need two wooden planks and two strings. When interacting with the loom, simply place in the banner the dye of your choice to color the pattern, or create or use a banner pattern item to copy the contents to a banner.

TIP

If you place a banner and a shield into a crafting table in *Minecraft Java Edition,* it applies the banner to your shield. This way, you can walk around proudly displaying your patterns and colors.

Building an Effective House or Base

Bases and houses are essential to the Minecraft experience: They are used to store your items, place a bed, and create projects and farms, among other tasks. Optimizing your base can introduce significant improvements to your world. Here are our tips to build an effective house or base:

- >> **Start small:** At the beginning of the game, bases don't have to be large. As you gain more resources and expand your world, you can always find room to grow your base. Starting small ensures that you don't feel stressed or overwhelmed about upgrading your base.

- >> **Develop structures:** Structures like farms or protective moats are helpful additions. Building structures around or in your base greatly improves it.

- >> **Use utility blocks:** Your base is where you should set up most utility blocks. You might create one room for smelting and another room for cooking food, or even create a lounge with a jukebox to play your favorite tunes.

- >> **Upgrade your base:** After building a base, you don't have to just leave it alone — you can expand it or even create separate buildings for specific tasks. That strategy helps keep you organized and is a fun way to play your world. In Figure 5-4, you can see an underground base we made that can be easily expanded on.

FIGURE 5-4: A base we made.

REMEMBER

Always consider our advice as only a suggestion or a guide to express yourself creatively — bases are up to you. If you don't want a large base, don't create a large base. In Minecraft, you get to choose how to build or explore.

Knowing Where to Store Items

Storage is a big part of building your base and gathering resources. You can handle only so many items in the inventory. When storing items in a simple double chest (see Chapter 3), sort the chest in a way to easily find items you need to access later. It's the worst feeling to have a messy chest where you can't find any of the items you stored.

Our favorite method of storage in the early game to midgame is to apply a theme to multiple chests, such as a chest dedicated to storing ores and valuable materials in mining and another one dedicated to storing dirt, cobblestone, and other miscellaneous materials while mining. You might have a chest for farming and another one for tools — the list can go on and on until you feel organized.

Later in the game, we build an entire room dedicated to storage. Whether it's underground or in our base, we still make it accessible and organized so that, after a long mining trip, we can go back and dump all our resources in an organized manner.

TIP

Barrels are useful storage blocks that are more aesthetically pleasing than chests. Barrels can be placed near a bedside, or even in walls to provide easy, hidden storage. We use barrels to hide our more valuable items and our more useful items for easy access later. Figure 5-5 shows a barrel in our house by our bedside.

FIGURE 5-5: A barrel by the bedside.

Chapter **6**
Exploring Biomes

All worlds have more than a single biome (as in real life), so you can gather resources as you move through the biomes. Because gathering wood is important early in the game, many players need to find a wood-based biome as soon as possible. In this chapter, we look at the staggering array of biomes (Minecraft has 60 of them) that you can explore. Then we take a look at farming and, finally, explore the various mob types.

Knowing What's What with Biomes

You have to know about the different types of biomes so that you know what to look for and how to build your Minecraft-related vocabulary. Table 6-1 describes the basic biomes.

REMEMBER

Knowing the biome names and what they do isn't as important as knowing how to benefit from biomes and knowing what they contain. Knowing where to obtain the different types of wood (see Chapter 5) can help you in building and decorating your own structures.

Cool ice biomes

Ice biomes are where you can obtain packed ice and blue ice. You move faster when running and jumping on packed ice and even more so on blue. They are aesthetically pleasing to look at and fun to explore.

TABLE 6-1 **Biomes**

Biome Name	Description
Badlands Wooded Badlands Eroded Badlands	The Badlands biomes contain dry, desert, rock-like structures, such as that of Zion National Park or Bryce Canyon National Park in the United States. Badlands biomes are our favorites, and we talk about them later in this chapter.
Birch Forest	Birch Forest biomes resemble normal Forest biomes, but with birch trees instead of oak.
Cold Ocean Deep Cold Ocean Deep Frozen Ocean Deep Lukewarm Ocean Deep Ocean Lukewarm Ocean Ocean River Warm Ocean	Oceans resemble the ones in real life, containing large bodies of water — frozen or not. The state of the ocean is dependent on the surrounding biomes, so if an ocean is connected to an icy biome, it's likely a cold or frozen ocean.
Dark Forest	The Dark Forest biome is a standard forest that contains larger trees, dark oak, mushrooms, and an overall darker look.
Desert	Filled with sand and cacti, the Desert biome is long, but it contains some interesting villages and structures.
Forest Flower Forest	The Forest biome is your standard tree-filled area containing oak trees. Flower Forest biomes are flower-covered Forest biomes with a little more room so that more flowers can grow.
Jungle Bamboo Jungle Sparse Jungle	The normal Jungle biome contains a thick, rainforest-like biome. Bamboo Jungle is the same as the basic Jungle biome, but with bamboo and pandas. The Sparse biome is a significantly less thick jungle with spread-out trees.

Biome Name	Description
Meadow	The Meadow biome is like a Plains biome, but is part of a mountain and with more flowers, which in turn causes more bees and beehives to spawn.
Mushroom Fields	The Mushroom Fields biome is a unique biome generated only around a deep ocean. This biome contains mycelium, which is a purple grass that helps mushroom growth. It's the reason that so many mushrooms generate on an island in the Mushroom Fields biome. It is also the exclusive home of the cow variant: the Mooshroom.
Plains Sunflower Plains Beach	These are the most basic Minecraft biomes, all containing flat and basic light green grass. Few trees spawn, and sunflowers only sometimes grow. Beaches are attached at the end of most biomes into the ocean.
Savanna Windswept Savanna Savanna Plateau	The Savanna biomes resemble those of an African forest, with widespread land areas and trees bearing few leaves. The grass even looks drier!
Snowy Beach/Plains Ice Spikes Frozen River/Ocean Jagged/ Frozen Peaks	These frozen biomes, which are mostly ice-covered, are useful for collecting packed ice and blue ice to move fast on. They don't contain much wood other than shipwrecks.
Stony Peaks	Stony Peaks is another one of our favorite biomes, creating large stone mountains that can carry snow at the top. This biome is one of the few that contains the goat.
Swamp Mangrove Swamp	The Swamp biome is a rarer biome that looks normal, like what you would expect. It's a darker, muggier environment that contains small pools of water. Trees grow here with lots of vines. A Mangrove Swamp biome is the same as a normal swamp, but is thick with mangrove trees and mud. Mangrove Swamps tend to spawn in warmer areas near desert and jungle biomes.
Taiga Old Growth Pine/Spruce Grove	The Taiga biome contains longer trees with a thick forest and a colder temperature. This biome has a darker theme to it. Grove biomes are Taiga biomes but are covered in snow.

In the midgame, when you need to travel quickly between biomes, packed ice and blue ice are useful ways to create highway systems. If you place a boat on ice and ride the boat, you travel 40 blocks per second; on blue ice, you ride approximately 73 blocks per second. In comparison to if you were to ride a boat in water, you would ride at 8 blocks per second; normal sprinting, you run approximately 6 blocks per second.

The jagged badlands

The Badlands biome, more commonly (and formerly) known as the Mesa biome, is a red-and-orange terracotta-covered biome. Badlands are not only based on the geography of the western United States but also contain special mineshafts (see Chapter 8) that have a lot of gold and gold ore inside mountains and base-level caves. This biome is a cool reference to the gold rush in early American history. Figure 6-1 shows off what one of these gold mines looks like.

FIGURE 6-1: Gold Mineshaft biome.

This biome is also the one that contains only red sand and terracotta. Red sand is an exclusive block, and you can make terracotta by smelting clay in a furnace.

The green jungle

Jungles are green and *thick*. They contain jungle trees, which are the largest trees in the game, with lots of vines and cocoa beans to harvest along the way. In a bamboo jungle, you can find lots of exclusive mobs.

PANDAS

Pandas are the most unique animals found in the jungle. They can have one of these seven personalities:

>> **Normal:** This type of panda lacks any special qualities. It acts normally and is colored normally.

>> **Lazy:** This type of panda lies on its back, it's slower than normal, and doesn't follow you in *Minecraft Java Edition* if you hold bamboo in your hand.

>> **Worried:** This type of panda avoids players and all hostile mobs, and it starts to shake and covers its face during a thunderstorm. It doesn't eat bamboo or cake on its own.

>> **Playful:** A playful panda rolls over and jumps around.

>> **Aggressive:** When this type gets hit by an attacker, it continues to attack that item until it dies — rather than attack the item just once. These pandas also become hostile if another panda nearby gets hit.

>> **Weak:** A weak panda sneezes more often when it's a baby, and it has half the health of a normal panda.

>> **Brown:** A brown panda's personality is the same as a normal panda, but instead of being black-and-white, it's brown-and-white.

PARROTS

Parrots, which are also unique to jungles, have special properties. They can be tamed with any kind of seed. See Chapter 7 for more info about taming parrots. After parrots are tamed, they can perch on your shoulder and imitate sounds of nearby mobs, but in a higher pitch. They also start to dance whenever music is played in a jukebox. Figure 6-2 shows off all the jungle goodness.

OCELOTS

Ocelots can be found only in bamboo jungles. Wild cats that can be tamed with raw cod or salmon, they run away from you if you walk toward them, so be slow — and quiet. Ocelots can be found in both editions of Minecraft in normal jungles but also in *Minecraft Bedrock Edition.*

FIGURE 6-2: A plethora of pandas, parrots, and ocelots.

Excavating Structures

Structures are an important part of exploring in Minecraft. Table 6-2 explains to you what each structure looks like and where to find it and examines the basics of the structure.

WARNING

Structures are dangerous — handle them with caution! If you aren't prepared to fight or move quickly, some of these structures can kill you easily. Be sure to wear armor, carry a shield, and wield your sword and carry a minimal number of items so that you don't lose your wealth.

TABLE 6-2 Structures, Structures Everywhere

Structure	Description
Desert Pyramid	Desert Pyramids, which are found in desert biomes, are large structures made from sandstone. If you dig in the middle of this structure, you see a large, 3x3 hole that has a pressure plate in the middle, at the bottom. Press it and it activates TNT to blow you up. If you successfully maneuver around the pressure plate, you can access four treasure chests!
Jungle Temple	Jungle Temples can be found in regular and bamboo jungles covered in moss and cobblestone. These structures contain two chests: one that's trapped that fires arrows at you and the other hidden but revealed after you solve a lever puzzle in the basement.

Structure	Description
Swamp Hut	Swamp Huts, which can be found in the Swamp biome, are small, wooden huts with a cauldron and a crafting table inside. They generate with one witch and one black cat that don't naturally despawn. The Swamp Huts continue to spawn witches after each witch dies.
Woodland Mansion	Woodland Mansions, which are the rarest of the structures found in the Dark Forest biome, are gigantic mansions with three floors and lots of rooms. They contain a lot of loot, but the loot is guarded by vindicators and evokers — which are some of the most difficult mobs in the game to defeat.
Ocean Monument	Ocean Monuments are made up of a turquoise, prismarine block and are found completely underwater, in any deep ocean biome. These structures have hostile mobs, guardians, and elder guardians defending each monument. Gaining eight blocks of gold is the main treasure of each monument, along with wet sponges, which can be obtained only through an ocean monument.
Shipwreck	Shipwrecks, which are found in all oceans and beaches, are wooden ships that have sunk. They can contain some treasure, maps to buried treasure, or just basic loot.
Igloo	Igloos, found in Snowy Plains or Snowy Taigas, can have a hidden basement underneath a carpet inside that contains a villager and a zombie villager locked behind bars. You can cure the zombie villager by way of a splash potion of weakness and a golden apple (see Chapter 9).
Ruined Portal	Ruined Portals can be found in any biome in the Overworld or the Nether. These portals are incomplete nether portals that often contain a chest that contains loot normally pertaining to gold. Chapter 11 goes into greater detail about Ruined Portals and Nether Portals.

3

Expanding Your Skills

Chapter **7**
Creating Farms in Your World

A fter you advance through the Stone Age and you develop basic food sources and weapons — in addition to gathering items from looting mobs — it's time to begin farming.

Farming in Minecraft is based largely on the type of biome your avatar spawned into at the beginning of the game. Some biomes lend themselves to mining earlier than farming, so you might want to read Chapter 8 first. Some types of farming and mob interaction are common in all biomes.

Working with Crops and Animals

As with natural history in the physical world, people are much more productive at farming than they are at hunting and foraging for food and other supplies. Minecraft lets you farm just as you would in the physical world, and you may be surprised at what you can learn as you begin to automate food processes.

Growing crops

Harvestable items such as wheat, melons, and pumpkins fit the raw definition of Minecraft farming by requiring well-irrigated farmland. Follow these general steps to set up a farm:

1. **Find a well-lit area made of grass or dirt.**

   If the area isn't well lit, craft some torches. A flat workspace makes this task easier, though it isn't mandatory.

2. **Craft a gardening hoe and use it.**

   You can interact with the ground to use the hoe to till farmland.

3. **Locate a water source nearby, and then interact with the water source while holding a bucket. Interact with the ground while holding the full bucket to dump the water near your crops.**

   Dig an irrigated hole or canal in your future farm, allowing any nearby farmland to thrive. Dry farmland grows more slowly and turns back into untilled dirt after too much time passes without crops being planted on it.

   The recipe for a bucket is the same as a bowl but with three iron ingots instead of sticks.

4. **Lock up your farm.**

   Jumping on farmland destroys it. Keep crops safe from animals and mobs by building walls around the crops. Fences and fence gates work well.

REMEMBER

Rabbits, in particular, can eat carrot crops quickly, so build a fence around your crops.

After these steps are finished, you're ready to harvest crops!

Farming wheat, carrots, potatoes, and beetroot

Wheat, carrots, potatoes, and beetroot are relatively simple to farm. Follow these steps:

1. **Collect seeds and vegetables.**

   Breaking tall or short grass blocks have a chance to produce a seed which is how your grow wheat. You can find carrots, potatoes, seeds or beetroot in villages, or zombies can sometimes drop carrots or potatoes.

2. **Interact with the farmland to plant seeds, carrots, potatoes, or beetroot.**

   Tiny green stems appear on the block.

ALEX'S
CORNER

   I like to find crops in villages.

3. **Wait until the crops are fully grown. Speed up this process by using bonemeal or artificial light, as described in this step.**

   Wheat is mostly yellow when it's fully grown, and carrots and potatoes are ready to harvest when the heads of the vegetables begin to emerge. Work on other tasks while you wait. You can also add bonemeal (crafted from skeleton bones) to grow crops instantly.

   Adding bonemeal to a crop by interacting with the crop with bonemeal in your main hand makes it grow one stage, significantly decreasing the growing time. Also, crops grow only with light. To supplement natural sunlight, place torches or other light-producing blocks around your farms.

4. **Break the crop blocks to obtain your profit.**

   Replant seeds, carrots, and potatoes until your farmland is refilled, and keep the remainder as profit.

Using this strategy, you can start a farm that obtains items for you while you enjoy the game.

TIP

Rather than place fence gates, you can place carpets on top of the fence. Mobs, including animals, don't see the carpet as a block they can jump on, but you can jump on the carpet to enter and exit your cropland. This strategy is particularly helpful when farming animals, because it prevents animals from leaving through a fence gate.

Harvesting melons and pumpkins

Growing large plants such as melons and pumpkins takes quite a bit of work. Follow these steps to start a farm like the one shown in Figure 7-1:

1. **Collect seeds.**

   You can find both melon and pumpkin seeds in treasure chests hidden in abandoned mineshafts. In addition, pumpkins found growing naturally in your world can be crafted into seeds. You can craft melon seeds from melon slices, which you can obtain by trading with villagers, as described in Chapter 9.

FIGURE 7-1: Growing melons and pumpkins.

2. **Interact with the farmland to plant seeds.**

   Unlike with wheat, farmland that allows you to plant melons and other large plants must be adjacent to grass or dirt. When these seeds grow into stalks, they tip over and grow melons or pumpkins next to them. To grow lots of melons or pumpkins, till a row of farmland next to a row of dirt and space water pools throughout.

3. **Wait for your harvest to grow.**

   You can use bonemeal on seeds to speed them into mature stalks, though the stalks won't bear fruit immediately. Pumpkins and melons just take awhile to grow. Ensure that these crops have plenty of growing space, and work on other tasks in the meantime.

4. **Harvest the crops.**

   To harvest pumpkins and melons, don't break the stalk blocks — instead, break the pumpkin and melon blocks that appear nearby. If you're harvesting pumpkins, you can craft them into pumpkin seeds to expand your farm. If you're harvesting melons, breaking the blocks produces melon slices that can be eaten or crafted into seeds.

Knowing the basic plants

The preceding section deals with the classic crops, which provides a good foundation in farming experience for most players in Minecraft. The next several sections, on the other hand, describe other growable items that can be exploited with farms.

Reaping sugar cane

Sugar cane consists of green reeds that grow naturally near bodies of water. Collecting at least one sugar cane block is enough to start a farm, like the one shown in Figure 7-2. Sugar cane is useful when produced in large quantities: Paper and items such as bookcases require lots of sugar cane reeds to craft. You can also make sugar for items such as cake and potions of swiftness with sugar cane.

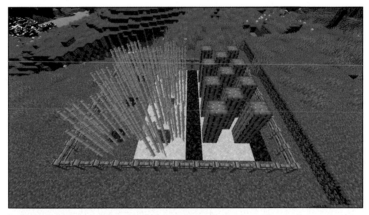

FIGURE 7-2: Growing sugar cane and cacti.

Fortunately, sugar cane is easy to farm. Just follow these steps to start farming it:

1. **Find (or make) a place that holds water.**

   Sugar cane reeds grow only near lakes or pools. They can grow only on grass, dirt, podzol, or sand.

2. **Place sugar cane blocks next to the water in the same way you would place any block.**

   When a patch of sugar cane reeds is placed where it can grow, it extends vertically until it's three blocks tall.

3. After the sugar cane is fully grown, harvest all but the bottom block.

When you break the stalk blocks in the middle, the top section breaks down into items. The reeds at the bottom begin growing again.

The essential concept is to plant a short patch of sugar cane reeds, let them grow, and then mow down the patch by harvesting all but the bottom blocks of sugar cane so that they can grow again.

TIP

When the ground is flat, you're at eye level with the point at which you should break the sugar cane reeds. Walk around with the crosshair at eye level while holding the Break Blocks button to break all sugar cane reeds quickly.

Utilizing cacti

Cacti are sharp desert plants that can be used for creating traps or for making green dye. (Refer to the small cactus farm shown on the right of the sugar cane shown earlier, in Figure 7-2.) You can typically find cacti in the desert, and you can grow them similarly to sugar cane (as described in the preceding section). However, growing cacti is unique because they

>> Require no water and must be placed on sand

>> Cannot be placed next to other blocks

>> Destroy items and hurt players touching them because they're sharp

TIP

Destroy the entire cactus and replant it to ensure that some of your profits aren't destroyed by other cactus blocks.

Enjoying cocoa beans

Cocoa beans, used to make brown dye, are an ingredient in cookies. The best way to find cocoa beans is to explore a jungle — the beans are found in pods growing on the trees. Though neither green nor yellow pods are fully matured, orange ones provide several cocoa beans when you smash them.

Farming cocoa beans is easy: To place a pod, interact with some jungle wood while holding cocoa beans. Then break the pod when it turns orange to harvest lots of cocoa beans. Make a large wall of jungle wood to start your farm.

Finding nether wart

You can find *nether wart* growing in special rooms in the nether fortress (described in Chapter 11). You can pick up nether wart by breaking fully grown crops. Nether wart is useful for brewing potions (described in Chapter 10). You can farm nether wart by planting it in soul sand blocks and waiting for it to grow, similarly to wheat (although you don't need to till soul sand the same way you till wheat).

Chopping down trees

Tree farms don't need to be created often — they're commonly useful when you live in a location with few trees nearby or when you want a wood source while underground. To grow trees, collect saplings — which are occasionally dropped when breaking leaf blocks — and then use the Interact button to place the sapling on dirt or grass in a well-lit area. (Remember that trees need lots of space to grow.)

TIP

Plant a square of four jungle saplings, dark oak saplings, or spruce saplings and apply bonemeal to one of them to make a giant tree grow.

Breaking bamboo

Bamboo can appear in the Bamboo Jungle biome (see Chapter 6). Bamboo blocks spawn and grow from the bottom, as many as 12 to 16 blocks tall. These blocks grow quite slowly — on average, growing once every 205 seconds. Bonemeal can be used, however, to grow bamboo taller by 1 or 2 blocks.

When you break bamboo, all bamboo above it automatically breaks as well. You can make a bamboo farm, similar to a sugar cane farm, but you don't need water to farm bamboo.

Finding glow berries and dripleaf

You can find *glow berries* or *dripleaf* underground in the Lush Caves biome (see Chapter 8). Glow berries hang from the ceiling of the caves in vines, with each block able to produce a glow berry.

When glow berries are ready to be harvested, little orange fruits appear on the vine. You can interact with these fruits, to get the fruit. You can make a farm by hanging glow berries from a post or any block.

Dripleaf, which you can find hanging around the caves, starts small and then grows to become large. You can use bonemeal on a small dripleaf to make it grow faster. When another mob is standing on a block of dripleaf and you stand on the mob, the mob drops under your weight after 1 second, which makes dripleaf useful for traps!

Savoring sweet berries

Sweet berries, which appear only in Taiga biomes, are a red fruit that's harvested from bushes. Like cacti, they're prickly and inflict damage if you touch — or another mob touches — the berry. You can still walk through a sweet berry bush, but it slows you down and deals damage to you.

When sweet berries are placed on the ground, a small bush appears that grows to become full. When the bush is ready to be harvested, red berries appear on the bush. Interact with the block to make the red berries drop without breaking the block. Just as you would pick berries in real life, sweet berries grow back without needing to be broken.

Attracting animals

You can use animal farms to acquire resources such as pork or wool without having to endure lots of hassle. Animals follow you while you're holding their favorite food. Interacting with two animals of the same species while holding their favorite food causes them to gain hearts over their heads and breed to make a baby animal.

Table 7-1 shows off the list of animals that can be tamed or that follow you when you hold their favorite food.

REMEMBER

A lamb's wool is the same color as its parents' wool. To farm a specific color of wool, interact with some sheep while holding dye to paint them, and then start a farm with them. Sheep regrow shorn wool by eating grass.

TABLE 7-1 **Breedable Mobs**

Animal	Favorite Food
Cow/mooshroom	Wheat
Sheep	Wheat
Goat	Wheat
Pig	Carrot, potato, or beetroot
Chicken	All seeds
Parrot	All seeds
Wolf	For breeding, any meat that isn't fish, cooked or uncooked, including rotten flesh. For taming, only bones can be used.
Cat/ocelot	Raw cod or salmon
Axolotl	Bucket of tropical fish
Llama	Hay bale
Rabbit	Dandelion, carrot, or golden carrot
Turtle	Seagrass
Panda	Bamboo
Fox	Sweet berries or glow berries
Bee	Any flower
Horse/donkey/mule	Golden apple, enchanted golden apple, or golden carrot

Growing mushrooms

Though mushrooms slowly spread if their climate is dark enough, the spacious, dark areas of a farm can attract monsters. If you don't want to have to perfect the lighting, use bonemeal on a planted mushroom so that it grows into a giant mushroom. Giant mushrooms can be used to quickly obtain lots of mushrooms when you break them. Because of the difficulty in providing enough lighting to prevent mobs but not too much to prevent mushrooms from growing, many players don't farm mushrooms or use mushrooms to farm mobs.

REMEMBER

Mobs don't spawn in the Mushroom Fields biome, allowing a player to farm mushrooms effectively. Mushroom fields are extremely rare, so take advantage whenever you see one.

Raising pets

A *dog* (which is a tamed wolf) is your noble companion — it fends off zombies from your base. Skeletons run away from dogs because the dogs know that skeletons are made of bones, and every dog loves a good bone! For that reason, it takes longer for a dog to kill a skeleton. Dogs don't go after creepers and if you have a dog with you, the creeper will still blow you up.

A *cat* can be found as a stray in villages — it likes the warmest places in your home. It sits on a bed or by a lit furnace or on your chest, making only the chest inaccessible. It doesn't get up unless it's pushed off that block. Cats often like exploring around players — when you sleep in a bed and have tamed a cat, it often goes to you and sleeps next to you. After waking up, the cat *might* bring you a gift, such as raw chicken, feathers, or other small animal drops. Creepers and phantoms that notice a cat run away from it.

The smallest of slime mobs can even count as a pet (see Figure 7-3). A slime is often cute, trying to fight against the big guy. It always follows you and tries to attack you, but because it is the weakest mob in the game (it has only half a heart), it causes no damage to you.

FIGURE 7-3: Pet slime looks like this.

Your horses define your place. Minecraft has 35 horse breeds (seven colors, five patterns). Horses have three different abilities, which makes them valuable:

>> How high they can jump

>> How fast they can run

>> How much health they possess

Horses can be tamed by riding them repeatedly until hearts appear. After you tame one, you can control it by putting a saddle on it. To tame a horse, open the inventory while riding the horse and place a saddle in the designated area that appears.

You can also find donkeys in the wild, which are tamed and act similarly to horses. They cannot run as fast, jump as high, or have higher health than a horse. The upside to them is you can attach a chest to them by holding the Sneak button while interacting with them with a chest in your main hand. After they have a chest, while riding them if you open up your inventory, you will see an area for storage that the donkey will hold and you can travel with.

Mules are the best of both worlds; if you breed a donkey with a horse, you get a mule. Mules have higher stats than donkeys, but lower than horses, but they can also carry a chest to store items in.

Setting Up Basic Farms

After you know how to manage animals and grow crops and maximize their properties, you can create an entire farm with them! Farms grow large easily, so starting small isn't a bad idea if you reinvest and don't let greed overcome you.

REMEMBER

If you want to live in your Minecraft world as a vegetarian, you can! You aren't required to own a farm with animals. Sheep's wool can come from shearing instead of killing, and golden carrots rein as the best food in the game.

Creating basic animal farms

Here's our guide to making the most basic farm that doesn't require lots of time or thought:

1. **Find an animal or two and lure it with its favorite food.**

   Animals follow you when you hold their favorite food in your hand. Your character walks faster than most animals do, so walk slowly and make sure you don't move too far ahead of it, or else it will lose interest.

2. Create a hole or fenced-off area to trap the animal.

Fences are helpful because animals can't jump over them, as seen in Figure 7-4. Holes are useful for temporarily holding an animal before moving it to a more specific facility.

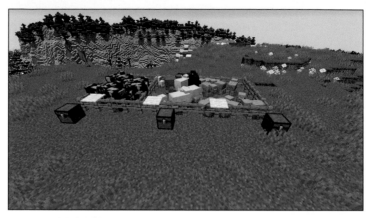

FIGURE 7-4: Animals in a pen.

3. Take the animal to the enclosure and let it start breeding!

The more animals you have in the enclosure, the more animals you can create.

4. When you've bred enough, kill some of the animals and collect the drops.

REMEMBER

Leave at least two animals left so you can breed a new herd!

Growing basic plant farms

Plant farms are useful when you're starting out — they can provide some easily obtained food for your world. When making any plant-related farm, we follow these basic guidelines:

>> **Create a compact farm.** On seed farms, just till the dirt, place water every eight blocks, and plant seeds between the water. On other types of farms, take a simpler approach and simply place a large quantity of the plant you want to grow in an easily accessible area.

>> **Reinvest in your farm.** Before you reap the rewards of creating farms and growing plants, be sure to replant crops and expand your farm so that you can easily have access to more of the plants you want to grow.

>> **Enclose your crops.** Choose a specific area for each type of crop and enclose them with a fence or similar block because animals can sometimes find their way into your farm and eat your crops or trample tilled dirt.

Creating a plant farm is a simple task that doesn't require a lot of effort. Expanding your crops and setting aside new areas for each farm occupies most of your time. But after the farm is up and running, the resources are limitless.

Automating Farms

Automation is our favorite part of farming, using basic redstone blocks or game mechanics to create automated farming systems. On an *automated* farm, you can automate basic tasks such as growing and harvesting food and plants or even create entire food- and resource-generating assembly lines! Before you understand how automation works, though, you need to understand the basic concept of redstone blocks.

Simplifying basic redstone blocks

Redstone is a complicated system that works a lot like electricity in real life. Redstone, which is collected from redstone ore (see Chapter 8), can be placed on most blocks to give power to blocks that are affected by redstone (meaning you can add redstone to those types of blocks). This section describes some blocks that are affected by redstone that are needed for automating farms.

Observing observers

An *observer* is a redstone block that produces a redstone signal whenever it "sees" a block update. A *block update* is simply a signal that specifies if anything changes about a block, such as growing a plant into a new stage, actuating a piston, or tilling a piece of dirt.

LEARNING ABOUT REDSTONE

Redstone isn't difficult to find — you can find this material frequently while mining. (Chapter 8 tells you more about mining.) Redstone's properties are quite simple: It is meant to work exactly like an electrical wire.

When you place redstone dust on the ground, it takes on a dark tone. When you place redstone dust next to other redstone dust, it connects and creates a line of redstone dust.

Redstone has an on–off position. When you place an item that can power redstone (a lever, redstone block, redstone torch, or button, for example) next to redstone dust, the redstone dust starts to faintly glow a brighter red, indicating that it has power. Redstone dust is used to connect to blocks (like the ones listed later in this section) to power each block so that it completes its intended task.

To power redstone dust, you must connect it into the specific redstone block and then turn on the redstone dust by way of a redstone power source to activate the redstone block. Typically, a redstone block remains in its intended state only when it's being powered — that is, it stops running whenever the power is off. Pistons are examples of these types of redstone blocks, which we talk about in the "Activating pistons" section.

Some redstone blocks cannot be switched again, however, until they first receive an Off signal. So these types of redstone blocks complete their action once and then wait for the redstone power to be turned off and then back on.

Observers have eyes on one side to observe the block update, and they output a signal on their opposite end. You can place a piece of redstone dust so that it's inserted into the opposite end of the observer, and then, when the observer views a block update, the redstone dust is briefly powered and lights up.

Activating pistons

A *piston* block is used to move or destroy blocks. When a piston is powered, the wooden end of the piston is extended, pushing (with certain exceptions) as many as 12 blocks in a row upward.

When unpowered, the piston is retracted and returns to its original state. When you create a sticky piston by combining a piston with a slimeball, it pushes the 12 blocks upward when powered, and when unpowered restores those 12 blocks to their original position.

Pistons also destroy plants if they "push" a plant, including melons and pumpkins. Plants also break if the block they're attached to is moved by a piston.

Dispensing dispensers

A *dispenser* is a block that, when powered with redstone blocks, throws, shoots, drops, uses, or activates items that are placed inside the dispenser. Dispensers drop items that aren't usable, but shoot items like arrows or snowballs when placed within.

In farming, when placing bonemeal inside a dispenser, the dispenser when powered uses the bonemeal on the block it's facing.

REMEMBER

The dispenser uses bonemeal only if bonemeal can be used, so if there's nothing to apply bonemeal to, or if a plant is fully grown, the dispenser makes bonemeal particles appear — but doesn't use any bonemeal.

Siphoning with hoppers

When an item is dropped on a *hopper* block, the item is added to the hopper's inventory. A hopper has a spout at the end. When connected to a chest or another storage block, the hopper automatically siphons all items in the hopper to the attached storage block. If a hopper receives power from redstone, the hopper doesn't siphon until the power source is turned off.

The direction in which a hopper siphons is determined by how you place the hopper. The direction of a hopper's siphon goes toward the block you place nearby. So, if you want to siphon into a chest, place it on or next to a chest.

Hoppers are useful for catching drops in automatic farms. This way, you don't have to manually pick up animal drops. To automate drop-catching, simply connect hoppers to a double chest and the drops automatically are placed in the chest.

All of these blocks can be seen in Figure 7-5. From left to right: hopper, dispenser, piston, and observer.

FIGURE 7-5: Redstone-powered blocks.

Building an automated plant farm

As new updates to Minecraft are released, automated plant farms become easier and easier to create. Some clever ideas have come out of these Minecraft updates, allowing better automation of your plant farm. This list describes the basic ideas for automating most plant farming:

» **Use observers to detect when a plant grows, sending a signal to pistons.** With observers facing either the root of the plant or a threshold of the plant, you can detect when the plant has grown. You can use this information to send a redstone signal, as shown in Figure 7-6, to pistons below to break the plant automatically.

» **Use water and a hopper for collection.** After you break the plant, the plant needs to be automatically collected. You can use water that leads into a hopper that leads into a chest that stores your plant for later collection.

For most plants, these two strategies work well, but not for wheat, carrots, potatoes, or beetroot. Unfortunately, you have no way to fully automate these plants using only redstone. However, you can make a semiautomated farm by following these steps:

1. **Create a large farm that gets elevated by one block every six blocks.**

    This step creates a bunch of farmland that you can place seeds on with water sources placed intermittently.

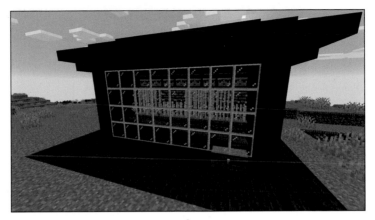

FIGURE 7-6: An automatic sugar cane farm.

2. **Place dispensers at the top of the staircases, filled with buckets of water.**

   Placing three or four dispensers does the trick. You activate them later.

3. **Connect redstone to all the dispensers to activate them all at one time.**

4. **Wait until the crops are fully grown and then activate the dispensers to have the water automatically destroy all the crops.**

   Make sure at the end that the collection location has flowing water and a hopper to a chest so that you can have easy access to your plants.

Building an automated animal farm

To automate animal farms, you need to know the size of the animal you're farming and the size of the baby version of that animal. Baby animals, when killed, don't drop anything, not even experience. Therefore, you must wait for the baby animal to grow up before killing it. The method for making an automatic pig, sheep, or cow farm is simple — follow these steps:

1. **Trap the animal that you want to farm in an enclosed, 1x2 area with water at the bottom.**

   Adult cows and sheep are 1 ½ blocks tall, so if they're in water in a 1x2 hole, they cannot jump out. You can still breed them, however, by holding the Interact button with wheat in your hand until the animal stops eating your wheat.

2. **Breed 20 animals.**

No more than 24 mobs at a time can occupy one block. If more than 24 mobs occupy a block, Minecraft kills the mob cluster until only 24 exist on the block.

3. **Set up a hole with a trapdoor on top connected to the initial hole.**

Baby cows, sheep, and pigs can fit through this hole, but the adults cannot. After breeding, the baby animal drops down into the hole, where you can kill it in Step 4. It's harsh — we know!

4. **Add lava, water, and a hopper connected to a chest.**

Add the lava one block above where the baby animal will end up. This way, when the baby animal grows, it will be killed by the lava automatically and (hopefully) humanely!

This step list isn't fully automatic, technically speaking, because you have to breed the animals yourself, but there's no way around breeding animals in an automated fashion.

REMEMBER

When an animal dies while it's on fire, the meat it drops is already cooked. (We can only hope that it's a fast, violence-free death!) Killing animals with lava relieves the need for cooking the animals. But be careful; if any items fall into lava, they get destroyed, including drops from animals!

» Making the most of mining

» Mining safely

Chapter **8**

Exploring the Minecraft Underground by Mining and Caving

Building your Minecraft empire requires that you explore and find all the necessary ingredients, ores, supplies, and food to be able to do everything you could possibly want. One basic aspect of exploring Minecraft is to build your own mines and extract all the necessary ores you need to build items in the game. The more advanced your mine, the more advanced your game becomes. When you want to do something more strategic than simply craft blocks and items, look to this chapter to find the basic techniques for mining ores.

Exploring the Mines

You must understand what you might be getting yourself into when mining. Minecraft has lots of dangerous situations you want to stay clear of so that you don't die with a lot of valuable resources. The next several sections describe the exclusives while mining.

Biomes

You can find three exclusive biomes while mining. To use these biomes more efficiently, you can read about cave mining in the following section.

Lush caves

Lush caves are small caves you might come across that spawn azalea bushes and trees. These caves also contain lots of moss and vines. The lush cave is the only biome to contain glow berries and axolotls when water pools are nearby.

Lush caves, whenever we make a cave base, are our go-to biome for building out a cave and adding our own spin. The glow berries and the similarity to a forest truly give these caves a fun twist. Figure 8-1 shows off a lush cave.

FIGURE 8-1: A lush cave.

Dripstone caves

Dripstone caves are also caves, similar to lush caves, that spawn in varying sizes. *Dripstone caves* contain dripstone blocks and pointed dripstone. Pointed dripstone is a spiky block that kills you or other mobs if it falls on your head or theirs.

Dripstone caves also contain massive stalagmites and stalactites, which are the same as the pointed dripstone, just like caves in real life! They're some of the coolest caves you can find in Minecraft.

Deep dark

The *deep dark* is a scary, dark cave that contains lots of mysteries to be discovered. Holding the ancient city (see the structures in the following section), these caves contain narrow corridors with dark blue sculk blocks found scattered across the ground.

The deep dark isn't an item that has been released in final form yet. It is now in the beta phases of testing, with some limited information being released for your use. This feature should be updated during the final edits of this book, when much more of version 1.19 is revealed.

Underground structures

Just like the Overworld, the underground has exclusive structures specific to that area. All these exclusive structures have loot and other goodies that can be found across the underground. Be sure to explore them with caution!

Abandoned mineshafts

Although abandoned mineshafts can also be found at the surface level inside badland biomes, they're more commonly found underground. An abandoned mineshaft can spawn anywhere in the underground — it's a mine full of mazes, with railroads running across the middle of each corridor, and support beams made of wood being used to keep the mineshaft secure.

At the end of hallways, or sometimes in the open, an abandoned mineshaft with a chest appears that contains loot.

WARNING

You can find cave spider spawners in abandoned mineshafts. They spawn cave spiders until the block is broken. Cave spiders are dangerous because, when they hit you, they deal a poison effect that hurts you no matter which armor or health you have.

ALEX'S CORNER

I like to put torches on the sides of a mob spawner to stop the spawner from spawning.

Dungeons

Dungeons are small cobblestone rooms that contain a spawner in the middle. The spawner in a dungeon is one of three types: zombie, skeleton, or regular spider spawner. The spawner works only if you get too close, though, and can be broken to stop spawning these mobs.

Each dungeon can have as many as two chests that contain loot. Dungeons are most commonly found underground connected to caves or connected to mineshafts.

Geodes

Geodes can be found only underground, but sometimes will spawn with the top aboveground commonly found on the sea bed, and contain no loot. They consist of three layers: an outer black layer made from basalt; a middle, white layer made from calcite; and an inner, hollow layer made from amethyst. Geodes usually spawn with a crack in them to make them stick out in caves, so you can find them easier.

Amethyst is the main resource to collect in geodes with the block and the crystals. Both parts of amethyst blocks are for decoration only and can't now be used to craft anything. Amethyst crystals give off a small amount of light, making it useful in builds with an ominous presence. Amethyst crystals can also be used to craft spyglasses, a fun tool to live out your pirate days!

Ancient City

The Ancient City is the largest structure in the game — and quite a scary one. Found in the deep dark, the Ancient City looks like a run-down city with a large structure in the middle. The Ancient City is used to create the warden, a boss in the game who is quite dangerous. We suggest not trying to fight the boss until much later in the game, after powering up, as explained in Chapter 10.

Other than the warden, the Ancient City contains lots of loot and cool features that are unique to the city. In the Ancient City, you can find skeleton heads, which are incredibly difficult to obtain otherwise, and some chests that have loot inside. The Ancient City is lots of fun to explore, but watch your step and be sure not to spawn the warden!

Mining Efficiently

Mining is an incredibly useful practice that gives you a fast (though challenging) means of obtaining strong minerals such as iron, gold, and diamond. You can mine in a number of ways, as described in this section, so use whichever method suits you best.

These mining tips aren't strict guidelines. Try your own methods, too!

Cave mining

Cave mining is challenging yet fruitful. To start, you must find a large cave — you can perhaps find one while working on another mine or exploring. If you find a large cave, you have a useful resource at your disposal!

Caves are generally *very* dark — and in Minecraft, darkness means monsters! Always be on your guard, carry weapons (and perhaps armor), and light up the cave with torches.

Cave mining is useful in growing your arsenal of resources and tools — by mining inside a cave, you can obtain many scattered resources without wearing out your tools trying to plow through stone or deepslate. Deepslate is an alternative to stone that appears very deep underground in your world. Ores spawn in both stone and deepslate, so keep an eye out for both types of ore when you're in these deep underground areas. Table 8-1 describes the various resources you can obtain while mining.

Caves can sometimes be deadly labyrinths, and you may lose your items if you die. You must decide whether the payoff in resources is worth the risk of losing them.

Benefitting from cave mining tips

When mining in a cave, use a torch or similar light source to light the way and skim the walls for minerals you can use. Iron ore is a common mineral to look for in caves, so, minimally, use this as an opportunity to collect iron ore while you're looking for other minerals in the cave.

If you mine deeply enough, you may find useful materials such as redstone, gold, and diamond. However, you may also come across lava — the bane of careless miners. Lava flows slowly and destroys dropped items (and you!), so avoid it and ensure that your precious ores don't fall anywhere near it.

TABLE 8-1 Mining Resources

Resource	Description
	Coal is an excellent resource for fuel in a furnace, or to make torches to light up your world and mines.
	Iron, which is useful in the middle of the game, is used to mine the rest of these resources.
	Copper is a fun resource, used mostly for decoration. It's used to craft a few useful items, such as lightning rods.
	Gold is useful for a lot of little items. It becomes much more useful in the Nether, as described in Chapter 11.
	Redstone is powerful — if you know how to use it. It's used to create electronic-like circuits.
	Emerald is rare but useful with villagers. It can't be used to craft anything except a block of emerald, but villagers love it (see Chapter 9).
	Diamonds are the best resource overall. Diamonds are extremely strong and used to make powerful tools. Be sure to pick up any diamonds you see.

Navigating ravines and canyons

Sometimes, while exploring or mining, you come across *ravines*. These narrow, deep gaps can appear underground or on the surface. Although ravines can contain lots of lava and monsters and are cumbersome to navigate, they expose a lot of surface area and are useful for finding minerals.

Ravines are helpful places to find iron and coal. Ravines are usually found on the surface, making them easy to spot. However, because they aren't deep, you cannot mine some types of valuable material, including diamonds, gold, and redstone.

A ravine also provides an excellent shelter because mobs cannot spawn on the walls of the ravine. You need to light the bottom around you by using torches.

TIP

If you enjoy mining and spend most of your time using a pickaxe, build a little rest area underground. You might want to include a bed, chests, and even a farm to provide you with food. Your house doesn't have to be located on grass.

Digging into branch mining

If you're new to Minecraft and you don't yet have the weaponry necessary to brave a cavern, branch mining is an effective way to obtain lots of stone and minerals.

Getting a handle on simple branch mining

Follow these steps to dig a simple branch mine:

1. **Dig your way underground.**

   You can dig any way you want, but don't dig straight down — you might fall into a pit, or into lava. A common technique is to use staircase mining, which is described in the later section "Stepping into staircase mining."

REMEMBER

   At the bottom of every world is a layer of unbreakable bedrock. Statistics have proven that the most valuable ore, diamond, is mostly located only a few blocks above this layer, so dig until your character has at least hit deepslate. Gold, iron, and coal, however, are mostly found in the stone layers above.

2. **Dig a tunnel.**

   The smallest tunnel that your character can fit into is one block wide and two blocks tall. Use torches to light the area, or else your tunnel will attract unwanted guests.

3. **Build more tunnels that branch off from the first one.**

   By building extra tunnels that split off from the main route, you can look for ores over a large area. Position the tunnels two blocks apart to be able to inspect a large surface area and not miss anything.

REMEMBER

Branch mining is effective because you can acquire lots of ores more efficiently. However, this type of mining consumes many tools because of the volume of stone you dig through. This style of mining produces, as a result, much more cobblestone than valuables. Branch mining is a helpful method if you have patience and a project in which you can invest your fortune of cobblestone.

Spinning into pinwheel branch mining

A simple way to set up a lot of branch mines is to use a pinwheel mine, as shown in Figure 8-2.

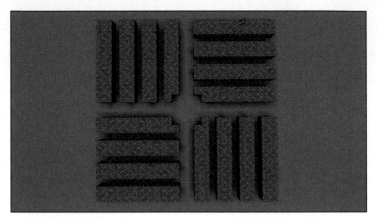

FIGURE 8-2: Pinwheel branch mine.

Follow these steps:

1. **Make a small 4x4 area.**

   Use this space as a staircase to reach the surface along with your chests, bed, and furnaces.

2. **Make 2x2 tunnels in all four directions.**

   This step determines how many branch mines you have, so dig a reasonably big tunnel. Make sure the tunnels are centered with your base. Dig one of the tunnels until the inventory is full.

3. **Make tunnels in the corridors you created in Step 2.**

   The spacing is up to you, but for maximum efficiency, place them about six spaces apart. If you want to be thorough, put them two spaces apart. Making the tunnel gets all the ores, for sure, but you might find that you've already collected all the ores from half of the tunnel. Keep digging until only three spaces remain in the inventory. Then head back.

Digging into tiered branch mining

The goal of tiered branch mining is to not miss a single ore in your branch mine. Tiered branch mining can be quite efficient at finding all the ore in a mine. Tiered branch mining is basically a strip mine, built on separate levels, as shown in Figure 8-3.

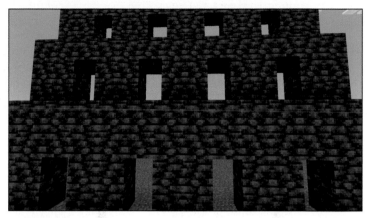

FIGURE 8-3: Tiered branch mine.

Follow these steps:

1. **Dig down to the level of the resource you want to collect.**

This is the base of your tunnels. Mining at lower levels gives you more access to diamonds.

2. **Dig four tunnels.**

Make sure that the four tunnels are 3 blocks apart. Dig one tunnel until your inventory is almost full. When coming back home, dig out all the ores you missed.

3. **Dig 4 blocks under the main shaft you made in Step 1.**

This is the second level of the branch mine.

4. **Dig another 16 blocks for the second shaft.**

The second main shaft is for another layer of the branch mine.

5. **Dig another four tunnels in the second shaft.**

This shaft should match the design and spacing of the first four tunnels. Where the first tunnels are above is where the second tunnels should be — below that.

6. **Repeat Steps 1–5.**

Repeat until you get down to bedrock. If this happens, lengthen the shafts to create more tunnels.

Stepping into staircase mining

In the staircase method, the goal is to dig deeply and quickly to do things like search for caves, find a suitable spot for a branch mine, search for minerals en route to destinations, or sometimes simply to build an attractive staircase (see Figure 8-3).

REMEMBER

Descend only one block at a time while staircase mining or else you can't get back up.

TIP

Craft stair blocks (wooden stairs, cobblestone stairs, and others are described in Chapter 5) to make the staircase ascension less taxing. (As Chapter 3 specifies, your character becomes hungry when jumping.) Raise the ceiling of the staircase to make your descent faster and less cramped.

ALEX'S CORNER

If you build a shelter on your first night, you can simply begin a staircase mine descending below your house. If you build this way, mobs cannot get in easily. However, they can still spawn unless you use torches, so be sure to create enough sticks and charcoal before the first night begins. I mine on the first night so that I don't waste my time waiting for daylight.

Many players build a staircase mine to Level -64 because those are the most diamond-rich levels. At that point, you would build a branch mine. However, you might encounter a cave before you reach those levels. You need to immediately light up the caves and kill the mobs within.

TIP

Caves are usually the most ore-rich, so don't miss the opportunity to mine inside of caves.

Building a quarry

A *quarry* is the simplest type of mining, and digging one is a useful way to gather lots of cobblestone — and to ensure that you don't miss any materials. To mine a quarry, dig a rectangle out of the ground, and then another one under it, and so on, until you have a sizeable hole from which you've unearthed every possible resource. Most players build a stairwell or ladder to exit and reenter the quarry. A natural and more efficient method is to use vines, which grow automatically (see Figure 8-4).

FIGURE 8-4: A classic quarry, for ascending and descending.

Although quarries produce lots of materials and can be mined safely, digging one requires great patience and generally isn't advisable. However, if you take that route, you can easily repurpose quarries into underground buildings.

Ripping into strip mining

An alternative version of quarry mining involves the use of TNT. Flattening out a large area on which to build your house is a form of strip mining. Another way to strip-mine is to flatten a giant mountain. The first five layers of the mountain consist of dirt and other elements. Placing TNT 2 blocks in the ground and 4 blocks apart should destroy the fifth layer, and a little of the sixth layer, of the mountain if all layers were dirt. After that, destroy one remaining layer at a time, 1 block by 1 block until you flatten the entire mountain.

Don't venture too close to the TNT after igniting it! TNT will kill you on a direct hit even with full iron armor!

Newer players often waste resources, especially tools, in mining inefficiently. They build elaborate branch mines, placing their tunnels too close together. Or they pick up ores that they already possess in large quantities. They also fail to bring enough food, weakening their players against mob attacks. Finally, new players don't usually bring enough weapons or armor to adequately protect themselves.

Rushing into speed mining

An expensive way to mine, but one used by advanced players, is to speed-mine. This is where you take advantage of the Haste II enchantment effect, which you create with a beacon and an efficiency 5 pickaxe, which you get from enchanting (see Chapter 11) to instantly mine stone. This isn't fast enough to mine ores, but it's fast enough to mine stone, allowing you to come back with a fortune pick (also from enchanting) and mine the ores you didn't mine out the first time around. Be sure to not move out of the beacon's effect range.

TECHNICAL STUFF

Within an hour and a half, the YouTuber Mumbo Jumbo (the name of a YouTube account featured in Chapter 12) mined 18 stacks of iron blocks (equating to 164 stacks of iron) using this method of mining.

Staying Safe While Mining

Mining is a dangerous activity that should be treated with caution, so here are some ways that we like to stay safe while mining.

Digging straight down

If you're ever in a rush and you want to simply dig straight down to find a cave, make sure to never dig in a 1x1 area. Always dig two at a time. By using this method, you don't dig and fall into a lava pool or fall into a big cave and die from fall damage or dig into a ravine that has a big drop.

Lighting the way

Making sure that mobs don't spawn, and that you can see clearly in dark areas, is vital to surviving and mining in Minecraft. If you can't see a skeleton or a zombie or you miss a resource, those mobs sneak up on you and can deal damage or kill you. Make sure you bring some torches as you're exploring in dark areas. Also, mine coal and bring it with you to make sure you can make more torches on your way.

Lighting up your caves also shows you a path to get back. Following the light in your cave allows you to see your way back to return to your base with ease. It also guarantees that when you return to that same cave, you won't be surrounded by mobs again and you can do something with that cave, without the worry of being attacked.

Attacking mobs

Knowing when to attack and when to run from mobs allows you to survive for much longer. Mobs will, without a doubt, appear and attack you while you're mining. Always make sure to keep a shield and a weapon on you, to defend yourself against angry mob attacks.

TIP

A shield is vital because it blocks all damage an enemy tries to inflict on you. Creepers are known for sneaking up on you, and sometimes even falling from ledges landing in front of you, so always have a shield with you that can quickly block damage from a creeper.

Chapter **9**
Leading Your Village

Trading in Villages

A *village* is a group of structures — such as hovels, smithies, churches, and roads — arranged as a community for its residents. A village can appear in a plains, savanna, desert, snowy, or taiga biome, all with their own unique features and buildings dependent on the biome. Villages spawn naturally in the world, and most people find them throughout the game.

A village can be an automated way to farm and increase your resources throughout the game. With many villagers at your disposal, you now have a workforce of villagers to tend to your crops and livestock. In addition, each villager has a profession and, by interacting with the villagers, you can trade emeralds with them for items in their possession and related to their profession that can help you in the game.

Exploring villager professions

Every villager has a profession. Professions determine how a villager looks and what they trade. For a villager to pick a profession, they must claim that profession's jobsite block, assuming that it's unclaimed. When the villager has claimed that jobsite block, which must be in the boundary of a village, they gain that job and the block's features. Table 9-1 describes every villager profession and jobsite block and spells out what each profession trades.

TABLE 9-1 **Villager Features**

Villager Profession	Jobsite Block	What They Trade
Armorer	Blast furnace	Chainmails or iron and various enchanting tiers of diamond armor
Butcher	Smoker	Meats, sweet berries, dried kelp blocks, and rabbit stew
Cartographer	Cartography table	Banner-related items and map-related items
Cleric	Brewing stand	Redstone dust, glowstone dust, and other potion-related items (because of a cleric's focus on potions), as described in Chapter 10
Farmer	Composter	Crops and plant foods, such as carrots and bread (but not meat)
Fisherman	Barrel	Fishing items such as fishing rods or campfire
Fletcher	Fletching table	Bows, crossbows, arrows, and other archery-related items
Leatherworker	Cauldron	Turtle scutes, rabbit hide, and leather-related items
Librarian	Lectern	Enchanted books, clocks, compasses, glass, ink sacs, lanterns, and other library-related items
Mason/ stonemason	Stonecutter	Terracotta, clay, quartz, and polished stones
Nitwit	None	None, because they're simply too dumb to learn a profession, for example, or do anything such as trade
Shepherd	Loom	Shears and wool from sheep but also dyes, paintings, and beds, which are wool-related
Toolsmith	Smithing table	The same as the weaponsmith (see the last bullet in this list) but with harvesting-related tools going as far down as to stone tools
Unemployed	None	Cannot trade until they have claimed a suitable jobsite block
Weaponsmith	Grindstone	Enchanted melee weapons and minerals

To turn a villager into a different profession, break the villager's jobsite block and place a new one near it for the villager to claim. You can do this outside of villages as well, if you want to set up farms with villagers inside. But villagers without a village lose some benefits and can't be bred easily.

Trading with emeralds

To trade with villagers, right-click them and use emeralds as currency to buy and sell materials. Though the most common villager is the farmer (wearing a brown robe), you have other trading options, such as butchers (white aprons), toolsmiths (black aprons), weaponsmiths (eyepatch), librarians (white robes), and clerics (purple robes).

To trade with villagers, follow these steps:

1. **Interact with a villager to open the Trade menu, as shown in Figure 9-1.**

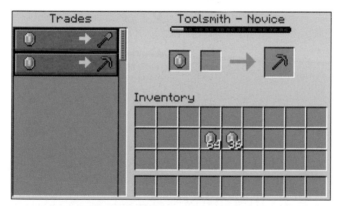

FIGURE 9-1: Trading inventory.

The top of the Trade menu shows a large, gray arrow with an item to the right and one or two items to the left. The items to the left of the arrow are the ones the villager wants. If the villager wants to buy materials such as raw meat or paper, find some. If they want to sell you items for emeralds, obtain some by selling to other villagers.

2. **Place the items that the villager wants in the corresponding slots on the Trade menu.**

   The item you want to buy appears on the right side of the menu.

3. **To accept the trade, take out the item that appears.**

4. **Close the Trade menu and wait for a moment. If green sparks appear around the villager (indicating that the villager has unlocked a new trade option), repeat Steps 1 through 3 to trade new items with the villager.**

   When you trade with the villager again, press the arrow buttons to cycle through available trades. Some trades close when you use them too many times or you harm the villager who is offering them.

5. **Find other trading opportunities.**

REMEMBER

   Villagers have professions (easily recognized by their clothing), which can be used to obtain more specific items. Be sure to acquire and upgrade professions in Minecraft that you need and that will help you progress in the game. You can acquire good diamond armor and tools simply by trading, so do your research and make sure you know what you're trading.

You can trade with villagers by using emeralds directly or by compiling a complex list of other trades to obtain emeralds, which are then used to buy other items you want.

Restoring a villager

Villagers can repopulate their own cultures, but sometimes an attack leaves an entire population devastated. Just as zombies in movies can infect humans, they can infect villagers! Have no fear, though: You can restore any zombie villager to their normal state.

To restore a villager, follow these steps:

1. **Find a zombie villager.**

   This type of villager burns in the daylight, so make sure that a few are indoors. A zombie villager wearing a helmet is also immune to daylight.

2. **Throw a splash potion of weakness at the zombie villager, and then promptly interact with the villager with a golden apple.**

   The effect from the potion lasts only briefly, so act swiftly with the golden apple. (Chapter 10 has the lowdown on potions.)

3. **Wait.**

   The zombie villager shakes slightly and emits red swirls, indicating that they're reverting. Wait it out for a minute or so and you have a villager.

If the new villagers can remain safe until the zombies have been either converted or slain, you will have restored a village to its former glory.

Gossiping

Villagers, when talking to others, can gossip based on what you have done to a villager. If you attack a villager — or kill one — the villagers talk to each other and raise prices. When trading with a villager, they sometimes discount their other items as well, encouraging you to buy or sell more to them.

If you cure a villager, they not only discount their own trades but also "tell other" villagers to discount as well. If you cure villagers more than once, discounts can become greater. Figure 9-2 shows off what a discount on items looks like.

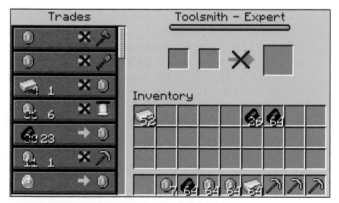

FIGURE 9-2: Discounted trades.

Trading Your Way to Wealth

The biggest issue with trading is how expensive it can become. One piece of diamond armor can cost up to 27 emeralds! The following four sections describe some ways to get wealthy.

Farming for farmers

The easiest trades made from farming are with farmers. At level 1, farmers start out being able to trade wheat, potatoes, or carrots for emeralds, but the real star of the show is unlocked at level 2.

After you can trade pumpkins for emeralds, the process of trading with farmers becomes much quicker because pumpkins grow much faster in farms. Most trades also require much less pumpkin per emerald than they do for wheat, potatoes, or carrots.

Farming sugarcane

Another farm you can easily make is a sugarcane farm, which produces a lot more than other plant farms do. Building a sugarcane farm allows you to turn sugarcane into paper and then trade the paper to a cartographer for emeralds.

Killing zombies

Minecraft lets you recycle almost every item you come across. For instance, did you ever wonder what you can do with all that rotten flesh from zombies you've killed in Minecraft? It turns out that you can trade rotten flesh to clerics for emeralds. If you find a zombie spawner in a dungeon, you can turn it into a zombie farm, which in turn gives you trades for clerics.

Clerics are especially good to trade with because one of the enchanted books they can sell is a mending book. It might not be a bad idea to take a villager with you to a farm and turn the villager into a cleric!

Shearing sheep

Another easy way to farm is to get a shepherd who trades wool for emeralds and find out what color of wool the shepherd wants to trade for. Then find sheep with that color of wool, or dye wool to get emeralds from the shepherd.

Raiding and Illagers

Another essential piece of villages is the antivillager, otherwise known as an illager. Illagers also have their own set of mobs that they control. Table 9-2 describes the various types of illagers.

TABLE 9-2 **Illagers**

Illager	Description
Pillager	Pillagers carry crossbows and are the only illagers found in outposts and patrols.
Vindicator	Vindicators are illagers that attack only with an iron axe. They appear in both woodland mansions and raids.
Evoker	Evokers are scary illagers that use spells to spawn vex (which is a flying mob similar to the phantom) and fangs that travel across the ground to attack you.
Ravager	Ravagers are large beasts that illagers can ride into battle, but they also attack on their own and inflict a lot of damage.

TIP

If you ever get into a tight spot with illagers, you can simply run away. Most aren't faster than you are when sprinting, so it isn't that hard to get away.

Locating illagers

The only illager you can find out in the wild is the pillager. Pillagers spawn around you in patrols, in a group of one to five pillagers, if you're outside of a village. Every patrol has a patrol captain, which is a pillager wearing an ominous banner. If you kill a pillager captain, you get the Bad Omen effect, which, in terms of gameplay, has no effect on you. (A little later in this chapter, we tell you more about the Bad Omen effect and raids.)

Pillagers also spawn in structures known as pillager outposts, which contain lots of pillagers and pillager captains. Each outpost consists of three floors with chests that contain loot interspersed throughout each floor. The outpost can also spawn a cage nearby with an iron golem stuck in the cage. If you break the iron golem free, he can help you defeat the outpost and gain the loot.

Raiding villages

When killing a pillager captain, you might notice an effect called Bad Omen placed on you for 100 minutes (or 5 game days). This effect, though it doesn't hurt you personally, causes a raid event if you walk into a village while the effect is still active.

REMEMBER

A raid is an event that spawns waves of illagers, as well as other mobs, that attack villages. You know that a raid is happening because the *boss* bar, labeled *Raid*, appears in the heads-up display (HUD) after walking into a village (see Figure 9-3). It's your decision whether to defend or run away from a village that's being raided.

FIGURE 9-3: Raid boss bar <insert dramatic music>.

Raids are specific between Java Edition and Bedrock Edition, so we're splitting the two for you, depending on which edition you're playing on.

If you're playing on Bedrock Edition

In Bedrock Edition, you experience only a single Bad Omen effect. Every raid is at the same level, so illagers don't spawn with enchanted weapons. Every raid has the same difficulty of mobs regardless of bad omen level.

The boss bar indicates how many mobs are left to be defeated. Depending on the difficulty of your game, a different number of waves appear. Easy level has 3, Normal level has 5, and Hard level has 7. A horn sounds at the beginning of each wave and continues to sound intermittently until the wave is defeated or you have died or lost the raid. In Bedrock Edition, pillagers and vindicators often drop additional loot, including iron armor, iron tools, emeralds, and enchanted books.

If you're playing on Java Edition

In Java Edition, the Bad Omen effect stacks up to Bad Omen V (5). Bad Omen V occurs whenever you're killing more pillager captains while the Bad Omen effect is still enabled. The first pillager captain killed gives Bad Omen I, if that is still active while killing another pillager captain you will receive Bad Omen II, and so on and so forth. Or, in outposts, the Bad Omen effect can naturally start at a higher level. The higher the Bad Omen effect is, the stronger the mobs are during raids.

The *boss bar* indicates how many mobs remain to be defeated. Depending on the difficulty of your game, a different number of waves appear on the boss bar. Easy mode has 3 waves, Normal mode has 5, and Hard mode has 7; or, if your Bad Omen is Level II (2) or higher, each difficulty level has an extra wave. Each Bad Omen difficulty level offers a range of mobs that can spawn during each wave. Based on the Bad Omen difficulty level, some raids might have more mobs spawn while other raids don't spawn as many mobs. Unfortunately, Java Edition doesn't include any special drops during raids.

Totems of undying

The biggest reason to start a raid is that — no matter what — an evoker that dies drops a totem of undying. If you hold a totem of undying in your off-hand (by placing it in your shield slot), when you die, the totem is used and an animation is played, healing you and causing you to live on.

Tips for defeating raids

Knowing about raids is half the battle of winning them. Next, we show you how to defeat raids — here are a few tips:

» **Enlist iron golems to help you fight!** Every village holds 1 iron golem that spawn naturally. Iron golems deal a lot of damage. As long as you don't attack an iron golem or a villager, iron golems attack only illagers. When iron golems are attacked, their skin starts to crack. Interact with iron golems by holding iron ingots to heal them, and then they can continue helping you attack illagers.

» **Use cobwebs and attack from a distance.** Another tactic you can use to fight illagers is to gather cobwebs when mining (see Chapter 8) by using sheers to harvest the cobwebs. Then place the cobwebs strategically in a place where illagers will get stuck in them, and shoot the captured illagers with a bow or crossbow.

» **Power up before starting.** Remember that raids start when you walk into villages, so get ready by healing yourself and making sure you have all the tools you need before you start one.

Chapter **10**

Powering Up with Weapons and Potions

O ne of the most exciting parts of playing Minecraft is your ability to power up weapons, tools, armor, and even yourself. This chapter explores the complex but rewarding aspect of enchantments, brewing, and beacons.

Many of the items we describe in this chapter can be achieved only after you have collected resources in the Nether (see Chapter 11) and earned a significant number of experience points (as reflected on the little green bar above the hotbar) by progressing through the game, killing mobs, collecting experience orbs, and completing other tasks. Alternatively, you may find items already enchanted in chests, dungeons, or other structures or even find potions dropped from a witch. And, sometimes you cannot gain other powers until overcoming certain obstacles in the game, like building a beacon.

Whatever your current status in the game currently, don't get discouraged! When you have gathered all the necessary resources to start enchanting and brewing your first potions, you will likely find enchantments and brewing to be rewarding experiences in Minecraft that are well worth your effort.

Enchanting Weapons, Tools, and Armor

To *enchant* means to add special powers to an item, making it more effective. For example, you can make a pickaxe mine faster or make a pair of boots that mitigates the damage inflicted from falling by enchanting those items.

Enchanting tables, used to enchant items, are crafted from diamond, obsidian, and a book (each of these ingredients is somewhat rare and takes time to gather, unless you switch to Creative mode). Generally, you need only one of these tables, which you place on the ground to begin enchanting. Don't worry about losing diamonds to enemies that might break your first enchanting table — enchanting tables are too durable to be destroyed by creepers or other hazards.

Enchanting an item

After you create an enchanting table, follow these steps to enchant an item:

1. **Interact with the enchanting table to open the Enchant menu.**

   The Enchant menu consists of 2 squares (where you can place the tool, weapon, or armor to enchant and where you place the lapis lazuli) and 3 tablet slots that show available enchantments.

2. **Place in the square the item you want to enchant and the lapis lazuli.**

   If the item can be enchanted, 3 tablets appear, each showing a green number (with the largest in the bottom row). This is the level of the enchantment — the green number above the experience bar represents the number of levels you must obtain to use the enchantments. Tablets appear grayed-out whenever you don't have the necessary lapis lazuli. Each tablet requires one more lapis than the previous tablet, with a maximum of 3 lapis needed.

3. **Select an available tablet to *ascribe* (or place an enchantment on) the selected item with a random enchantment.**

The higher the number on the tablet, the higher the chance of obtaining a powerful enchantment! But when you enchant, the enchantment uses only 1, 2, or 3 levels, based on the tablet you chose — the one in the highest slot, costing 1 level, and the lowest slot, costing 3 levels.

Tablets can reach Level 30 to provide especially strong enchantments. Unfortunately, if the enchanting table is placed without bookshelves, you can't surpass Level 8. If you have a lot of experience with orbs and you want the best of the best, you have to power up the enchanting table.

To improve the enchanting table, place bookshelves nearby. When a bookshelf is near an enchanting table, the table absorbs information from the bookshelf and produces higher-level tablets. Bookshelves must be arranged in a certain way, however: As many as 32 bookshelves can be placed around a single enchanting table, as shown in Figure 10-1.

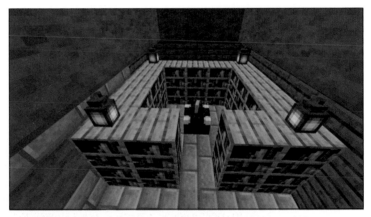

FIGURE 10-1: A powerful enchanting table in our underground base.

Only 15 bookshelves are required in order to access a Level 30 tablet, and you can subtract more if you lack experience orbs. To get 15 bookshelves, however, you must harvest 135 sugarcanes and kill approximately 45 cows. Ascribing low-level enchantments to some items while you get more bookshelves can be worthwhile.

Many players build houses large enough to hold their bookshelves and enchanting tables. Though enchanting tables are durable, bookshelves are not. To host a large number of bookshelves, you must be a savvy player and build a house using quality materials or build your house underground (refer to Figure 10-3).

Benefiting from enchantments

Whenever an item is enchanted, the item shows the names of all its enchantments under the item label. Some enchantments are followed by Roman numerals (such as I, II, III, IV, or V), representing the level of that enchantment. Enchantments are passive and take effect when you use the enchanted item. Available enchantments are detailed in Tables 10-1 through Table 10-5.

TABLE 10-1 Enchantments: Pickaxe, Axe, Shovel

Enchantment	Possible Levels	Effect
Efficiency	I, II, III, IV, V	The tool breaks blocks much faster than does a normal tool. On an axe, it also provides a higher chance of disabling a shield.
Fortune	I, II, III	Any block that cannot be replaced when broken, such as an ore or a melon block, has a chance of giving up extra loot. Gravel has a better chance of providing flint when broken.
Silk touch	I	This special enchantment lets you obtain any block you break as an item, even if it would normally drop another item, such as coal ore or stone. A silk touch item cannot be enchanted with fortune at the same time, and the item cannot harvest certain, blocks such as monster spawners.

TIP

When using fire aspect on a sword and killing animals, the animal drops cooked meat instead of raw meat.

TABLE 10-2 Enchantments: Sword

Enchantment	Possible Levels	Effect
Sharpness, smite, bane of arthropods	I, II, III, IV, V	These enchantments boost the sword's damage and cannot be active at the same time. Smite deals extra damage to the undead, and the bane of arthropods deals extra damage to bugs and causes slowness. Sharpness inflicts slightly less extra damage.
Knockback	I, II	Attacking an entity with this enchantment knocks it backward much farther than in a normal attack.
Looting	I, II, III	Mobs slayed with this sword can drop more items, and they have a higher chance of rewarding you with rare items.
Fire Aspect	I, II	Mobs that are hit with this sword are lit on fire and take constant damage over time.
Sweeping Edge	I, II, III	In Java Edition only, it increases sweeping damage when hitting a mob that is close to other mobs.

TABLE 10-3 Enchantments: Armor

Enchantment	Possible Levels	Effect
(Fire/blast/projectile) Protection	I, II, III, IV	Only one protection enchantment at a time can be used. The enchantment increases the defensive capacity of the armor. Four types of this enchantment can guard you against burning, explosions, or ranged weapons — the classic protection enchantment protects against all damage.
Thorns	I, II, III	When you get hit by a creature, this enchantment sometimes inflicts damage in return. A higher-level enchantment gives a higher chance of dealing damage.
Respiration (helmet only)	I, II, III	You can hold your breath underwater much longer while wearing this enchanted helmet.

(continued)

TABLE 10-3 *(continued)*

Enchantment	Possible Levels	Effect
Aqua affinity (helmet only)	I	Normally, you break blocks much slower while underwater. You can break underwater blocks much faster by wearing this enchanted helmet.
Feather falling (boots only)	I, II, III, IV	These enchanted boots let you absorb less damage from falling.
Depth strider (boots only)	I, II, III	This enchantment lets you move much faster in the water.
Frost walker	I, II	The frost walker turns source water blocks beneath you into ice until you step off, allowing you to walk on lakes.
Soul speed	I, II, III	Soul speed increases your walking speed when walking on soul sand and soul soil (see Chapter 11).

TABLE 10-4 Enchantments: Bow, Crossbow

Enchantment	Possible Levels	Effect
Power (bow)	I, II, III, IV	Arrows fired by this enchanted bow inflict bonus damage.
Punch (bow)	I, II	This enchanted bow is extra strong, knocking its targets backward.
Flame (bow)	I	Arrows fired by this enchanted bow are ignited and can set targets on fire, inflicting damage over time.
Infinity (bow)	I	This enchanted bow doesn't consume ammunition, so you can use it as long as you have at least one arrow. You can't retrieve arrows fired by this bow.
Quick charge (crossbow)	I, II, III	The quick charge decreases the loading time of a crossbow.

Enchantment	Possible Levels	Effect
Multishot (crossbow)	I	The multishot shoots 3 projectiles instead of 1 while still using only 1 projectile.
Piercing (crossbow)	I, II, III, IV	A projectile shot with this enchanted crossbow pierces through the mob, possibly inflicting damage on a mob behind your target mob, allowing you to kill up to 5 mobs at a time.

TABLE 10-5 **Enchantments Used on Anything**

Enchantment	Possible Levels	Effect
Unbreaking	I, II, III	This enchanted equipment is more durable and breaks much slower.
Mending	I	This enchanted piece of equipment heals durability when being held or worn while gaining experience.

Some powerful enchantments have several of these effects. For example, you might obtain a pickaxe with efficiency IV, unbreaking II, and fortune I. You can combine enchanted items using an anvil if you don't get the enchantment you want and you want to improve your enchantment.

Repairing items on the anvil

The anvil can repair, combine, and name items. You can place two damaged tools on the Crafting grid to combine their durability, though placing them on an anvil allows you to keep your enchants the item has. Place an anvil on the ground and interact with it to open the menu, as shown in Figure 10-2.

FIGURE 10-2: The Anvil menu.

To repair a tool, weapon, or piece of armor, place the item in the leftmost slot on the menu. In the middle slot, add base materials. For example, to repair wood, you need planks; similarly, you can use leather, cobblestone, iron ingots, gold ingots, or diamonds for items that use those materials. In exchange for experience levels (indicated by the green number that appears at the bottom of the screen after you find a certain number of experience orbs), the anvil increases the durability of a damaged item. Each material can repair only 25 percent of the durability of the item. Enchanted items remain enchanted.

In addition, you can place a second item of the same type in the middle slot on the screen to, in effect, combine the items. This action deducts more experience orbs than a normal repair action but allows you to combine enchantments and make those enchantments even more powerful. Also, certain items cannot be repaired using a raw material, including bows and shears. They can be repaired only by placing a sacrifice item in the second slot. The sacrifice item must match the target item exactly. For example, an iron sword cannot be repaired with a golden sword.

Unlike raw materials, which can increase durability by only 25 percent, combining two items using an anvil combine the durability of the two items together and then adds up to a 5 percent bonus. However, the durability can never reach more than 100 percent. Unless a player is seeking to combine enchantments, it would be a poor use of resources to combine items with durability over 50 percent.

To determine what a final repaired (or combined) item will look like, place the target item in the first slot and the sacrifice item (or material) in the second slot. The final item is displayed on the far right end, assuming that you have enough experience levels (or are playing in Creative mode). If you choose to complete the repair (therefore giving up the sacrifice item and experience points), place the final item in the inventory slot, finishing the anvil repair.

Rather than place a raw material or sacrifice item, place an enchantment book in the sacrifice slot, transferring enchantment to the target object. Two enchantment books can also be combined to create a higher-level enchanted book.

Not all enchantments can be combined. Enchantments that are considered contradictory or too similar cannot be combined, such as fortune with silk touch.

Anvils lose durability over time by repairing items (or by absorbing fall damage). Intentionally dropping anvils — though effective in killing mobs and producing a comical sight in Creative mode — generally isn't a good use of iron in Survival mode. An anvil can repair approximately 25 items before losing durability.

REMEMBER

Crafting an anvil requires 31 iron ingots. A complete set of iron armor requires only 24 iron ingots.

Finally, when you place any item in the leftmost slot, its name appears at the top — you can change it to whatever you want at the cost of a level. Your diamond sword can become Excalibur, for example, or a stack of saplings can become Minitree 6000s.

The name tag, a special item in Minecraft, works with an anvil. Name tags are found in dungeon chests, from fishing, or by trading with librarians. Name tags are rare. After you obtain a name tag, place it into the anvil and give it a name (like renaming an item). The name tag can then be applied to a mob. In addition to naming mobs for amusement, named mobs don't despawn, even when a player is some distance from the mob.

REMEMBER

Only hostile mobs despawn, so the name tag advantage is limited to hostile mobs. All mobs — even villagers — can be named except ender dragons and players.

TIP

Be on the lookout for a few Easter egg name tags. The two most common are Dinnerbone and Grumm, which make a mob turn upside-down, as shown in Figure 10-3. When naming a sheep Jeb_, its wool changes from a single color into a rainbow.

Brewing Potions

Brewing potions is another faculty available to you as you progress in Minecraft. After you obtain a blaze rod, which is a difficult item achieved in the Nether (see Chapter 11), you can craft it with cobblestone to make a *brewing stand*. This item is used to mix and set potions, which you can drink or throw to cause various effects.

To create a considerable number of potions, you need a good supply of glass blocks, a water supply, and nether wart. To craft glass, smelt sand in a furnace. Find nether wart in nether fortresses, and then farm the nether wart, as explained in Chapter 11. If you place the brewing stand in the Nether, you should keep buckets of water in the inventory. Glass bottles filled with water do not stack.

FIGURE 10-3: The name tag Grumm creates a horse that runs upside-down.

TIP

Build a brewing stand near your nether wart farm so that you can get all the nether wart you need.

When brewing negative potions, you need a large supply of fermented spider eyes. It takes time in the game to defeat enough spiders (or cave spiders) to gather this ingredient.

Brewing basic potions

Each potion begins by making a base potion and then adding an ingredient to create an active potion. Additional ingredients can be added to make a potion more intense, last longer, or turn negative. Finally, gunpowder can be added to create a splash potion.

To brew potions, follow these steps:

1. **Craft glass into bottles, and then interact with a water source or a cauldron to fill them with water.**

   These bottles can be brewed into potions. Craft enough bottles to make all the potions you want. A cauldron runs out of water quickly — a more effective option is a water block or buckets of water.

2. **Interact with the brewing stand and place some water bottles in the slots.**

   Because each ingredient yields 3 bottles' worth of potion, a savvy brew master always brews in groups of 3, for maximum efficiency.

3. **Add the base ingredient.**

   You usually add nether wart as the base ingredient, but you can add a fermented spider eye if you want to make a potion of weakness (described later in this section). When nether wart is added to water bottles, the result is an awkward potion.

REMEMBER

Blaze powder is used as a fuel to power the brewing stand. Make sure to get extra blaze powder to power the brewing stand and to use later as a potion ingredient.

4. **Add the secondary ingredients.**

   If you used nether wart, the water bottles turn into awkward potions, which have no effect. You can keep these awkward potions on the brewing stand, however, and add more ingredients to give them the additional characteristics you need; see Table 10-6.

Some of the figures in this book were produced by using the night vision potion (brewed from a golden carrot).

Using potions

To use a potion, select the potion and hold down the Interact button as though you're eating food. Though potions of healing have an instantaneous effect, others can last for a couple of minutes. Any potion effects you might have are shown when you open the inventory screen.

TIP

If you're afflicted with an effect such as wither or weakness, which can be dangerous, drink a bucket of milk to cleanse all potion effects. You can obtain milk by selecting a bucket and interacting with a cow.

TABLE 10-6 Basic Potions

Ingredient	Potion	Effect
Glistering melon	Potion of healing	Some health is restored.
Blaze powder	Potion of strength	You inflict more damage under this effect.
Ghast tear	Potion of regeneration	Your health rapidly regenerates.
Sugar	Potion of swiftness	You can run much faster.
Magma cream	Potion of fire resistance	You take much less damage from fire. This potion is a good one to use while fighting blaze.
Golden carrot	Potion of night vision	You can see much better in the dark.
Spider eye	Potion of poison	Damage is dealt to you over time; it's useless for now.
Fermented spider eye	Potion of weakness	Your attack power is reduced temporarily; it's useless for now.
Pufferfish	Potion of water breathing	You do not lose oxygen bar points when underwater.
Rabbit's foot	Potion of leaping	You can jump half a block higher.

Modifying potions

After you brew some potions, you may want to modify their effects. You can brew four different ingredients into the potions to modify them:

>> **Redstone dust:** Increases the duration of a non-instantaneous potion, allowing you to retain its effects for a long time. Redstone dust cancels out the effects of glowstone, described in the next bullet.

>> **Glowstone dust:** Makes potions stronger and more effective, if possible. Glowstone dust cancels out the effects of redstone (see Figure 10-4).

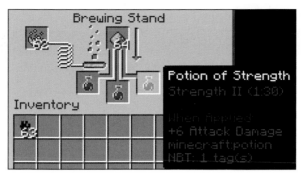

FIGURE 10-4: Potion of strength.

> **≫ Gunpowder:** Turns potions into *splash potions*, which have a differently shaped bottle. You can throw these potions by interacting with them. Whenever a splash potion hits an object, it explodes, applying the potion's effect to everything nearby. See the "Brewing splash potions" section, later in this chapter, for more information.

> **≫ Fermented spider eye:** Used on a potion with a positive effect, fermented spider eye reverses the effect, as explained in the next section.

Brewing negative potions

In addition to the helpful potions described earlier in this chapter, Minecraft has a whole class of negative potions, which generally have a negative effect on your character. You can make and use negative potions by adding a fermented spider eye to potions, as described in Table 10-7. Fermented spider eyes are crafted by placing a spider eye, sugar, and a brown mushroom anywhere on the Crafting grid.

As with other potions, these potions can be modified with redstone, glowstone, or gunpowder. As Tables 10-6 and 10-7 show, Minecraft has more types of positive potions than negative ones. To create a negative potion such as weakness, choose from more than one brewing recipe. Determine which ingredients are easiest and brew accordingly.

TABLE 10-7 **Brewing Negative Potions**

Negative Potion	Reagent	Effect
Potion of slowness	Potion of swiftness or fire resistance	You walk much slower.
Potion of harming	Potion of healing or poison	This potion instantly deals damage.
Potion of weakness	Potion of strength or regeneration or leaping	This potion reduces your attack power. However, you can brew it by simply adding a fermented spider eye to a water bottle.
Potion of invisibility	Potion of night vision	You become invisible, and you cannot be seen by anything unless you're wearing armor.
Potion of poison	Awkward potion	You are poisoned, damaging your health hearts.

The potion of invisibility is considered desirable by many players. It's considered a negative potion only because the potion of invisibility is the *corrupt* version: This potion is brewed by adding a fermented spider eye to a positive version of the night vision potion. When the invisibility potion is used, the player becomes invisible to other players and mobs. Beware: If you're wearing armor, you can still be seen!

TIP

To brew a potion of weakness, place a fermented spider eye into the top of the brewing stand with water bottles below, which creates an active potion with no additional ingredients.

Brewing splash potions

Some potions may seem useless because their effect on you is negative. When using a splash potion, you can instantly apply potions to anything you want. Simply brew gunpowder into any potion and it becomes a powerful projectile that you can throw by selecting it and interacting. Splash potions are slightly weaker their drinkable counterparts, but still are useful for several reasons, including these:

>> If you craft splash potions of healing, you can throw them on the ground to instantly heal yourself (and everything around you).

>> You can throw splash potions of slowness into a group of enemies to make a quick escape or use potions of harming to bring them down.

Splash potions can also be thrown using a dispenser (see Chapter 7).

REMEMBER

The order of ingredients in Minecraft matters significantly. For instance, if nether wart isn't added as the first ingredient to water bottles, the only potion that can result is ultimately a potion of weakness (created after a fermented spider eye is added).

Chapter **11**

Advancing to the Nether, The End, and Beyond

When you're all powered up and ready to fight any enemy that faces you, it's time to face the toughest challenges remaining in Minecraft. The Nether, a place covered in lava and mobs that are trying to kill you, and The End, the home of the ender dragon (the "final boss" of your Minecraft world), are the ultimate achievements, which you'll want to unlock in your Minecraft adventures.

Reaching the Nether

Finding the Nether is one of the first, and most difficult, steps in gaining access to the valuable loot that can be found only in the Nether. To reach the Nether, you must first create a nether portal.

A *portal* is a gateway that takes you to a new dimension in Minecraft, and it's named according to the destination that they take you to. For example, nether portal I leads you to the Nether, and the end portal leads you to The End.

Making the nether portal

A nether portal is built using a minimum of 10 obsidian, shown in Figure 11-1. Be aware that when you build the portal, the corners of the nether portal don't need to be filled, yet Minecraft automatically fills those corners when it creates the portal with your materials.

FIGURE 11-1: A nether portal.

To make a nether portal, place obsidian as shown in Figure 11-1, and then use flint and steel to light on fire any of the obsidian inside the portal you're building. Flint and steel are crafted by using 1 flint (randomly dropped after breaking gravel) and 1 iron ingot. After lighting the obsidian on fire, a purple, translucent portal appears between the obsidian.

You can also expand nether portals by making the portal longer or wider. If the portal is closed and larger than the portal shown in Figure 11-1, you can make a portal that is as large as 23x23 blocks.

Finding ruined portals

Another easy way to reach the Nether is to find a ruined portal. (We describe ruined portals briefly in Chapter 6, in case you want to learn a little more about them.)

Ruined portals are mostly finished nether portals with holes in the obsidian that's used to create them. Sometimes, a chest next to this type of portal contains the necessary obsidian to complete the ruined portal. They can also contain crying obsidian, a block that looks like obsidian with cracks, that will need to be replaced with normal obsidian in order to be constructed into a portal.

Proceed into the Nether with heavy caution! The Nether is an extremely dangerous place, and you should go there only when you think you can sufficiently defend yourself against hostile mobs and then explore the Nether biome without dying.

Entering the Nether

To enter the Nether, step into the purple portal you created in the previous section and then wait until you're transported. Following transport, you load into the Nether. Minecraft automatically generates a portal back to where you came from in the Nether, so you can return at any time.

The portal you came out of is one of the few ways to return to the Overworld, so remember the location of the portal! Don't worry if you forget, though: You can also bring enough materials to make another portal back to the Overworld, further on in the Nether.

Understanding the Nether's biomes

The Nether and all its biomes are considered dry biomes, so water is nonexistent in the Nether. Any ice you bring with you to the Nether can be placed anywhere in the Nether, but the ice just disappears after melting. In fact, packed ice and blue packed ice don't even melt in the Nether. Table 11-1 details all the Nether biomes.

When traversing these Nether biomes, take it slow until you have a good feel for the enemies and biome structures. Find good hiding spots, in case you need to run or dig into the wall!

Placing nether blocks

The Nether contains blocks that are almost entirely exclusive to the nether dimension. Table 11-2 describes the blocks you should know about mining in the Nether.

These blocks can be obtained only in the Nether, so keep an eye out if you want to use them in the Overworld.

TABLE 11-1 The Nether Biomes

Biome	Description
Nether Wastes	Your run-of-the-mill Nether biome. This biome has large open areas with lots of netherrack and lava. This is where you'll most commonly find nether fortress and bastion remnants (see the section "Exploring the nether structures").
Soul Sand Valley	A large, long, open valley filled with basalt, soul sand, and soul soil. Soul speed enchantments, as described in Chapter 10, are quite useful for quickly traversing the valley.
Crimson Forest	A crimson-themed biome (it's obvious for the Nether) with tree-like structures known as huge fungus. Crimson Forests contain red huge fungus. Crimson stems are the log equivalent of the tree.
Warped Forest	A dark, blue-green-themed biome. The Warped Forest biome acts identically to the Crimson Forest, but with a dark blue-green theme to it. This biome also has a grass equivalent called warped nylium. Endermen are the only mob that can spawn in this biome.
Basalt Deltas	A basalt-themed biome, modeled after the remnants of an ancient volcanic eruption. For this reason, the deltas have uneven ground, making it difficult to traverse. Basalt deltas contain little pockets of lava, so watch out!

Growing nether trees

In the Crimson Forest and Warped Forest biomes are two types of trees known as huge fungus. Each tree's trunks, which are known as *stems*, act the same as wood logs. The logs can be turned into their respective planks and used in place of any planks in crafting recipes.

Each huge fungus can grow shroomlight blocks near the top, which are light–emitting blocks. Huge fungus is used to create buildings. These blocks are a useful way to creatively light up your structures.

The sapling equivalent of a huge fungus is *crimson fungus* or *warped fungus*. These resources can be grown only on other crimson nylium or warped nylium. These blocks, in the Nether, work similarly to dirt in the Overworld.

TABLE 11-2 **Important Nether Block**

Block	Description
Netherrack	Netherrack is all around you in the Nether, with its red, rocky texture that is perfect for the Nether. Netherrack has little purpose or use in the game, other than as an easy way to obtain blocks to build bridges in the Nether.
Basalt	Basalt, which is a basic, darker stone, is a helpful building block for darker-themed builds.
Magma block	This block looks like netherrack, though lava flows through its cracks. This resource damages you or other mobs when you or they stand on a netherrack block — but unlike cactus, netherrack doesn't get rid of dropped items it touches.
Soul sand/soul soil	Soul sand slows down mobs and players who are walking on it, but soul soil does not. When a fire is ignited on either block, the fire emits a blue flame rather than the usual orange.
Nether quartz ore	Mining nether quartz ore is how you obtain quartz in Minecraft. Quartz is a useful building block for crafting certain redstone-based blocks.
Nether gold ore	You can obtain gold, as well as nether gold ore, in the Nether. Rather than give you raw gold, it drops golden nuggets. Placing 9 golden nuggets on a crafting table creates 1 golden ingot.
Ancient debris	Ancient debris is a late-game block that's used to obtain netherite ingots, the most powerful tools in the game. Netherite is talked about later in this chapter.
Glowstone	Glowstone is a glowing block that can be found in blobs attached to the roof of the Nether. When broken with a normal pickaxe, these blobs drop 2–4 glowstone dust; 4 glowstone dust can be crafted in the inventory to make glowstone.

To grow crimson fungus or warped fungus, place or find a fungus on the same type of nylium. To be able to grow, crimson fungus must be placed on crimson nylium, and warped fungus must be placed on warped nylium. After crimson or warped fungus is placed on any of these blocks, the only way to make these fungi grow — unlike the dirt-rooted plants and fungi in the Overworld — is by using bonemeal. Huge fungus doesn't grow on its own.

Distinguishing the various mobs

You have to know the mobs of the Nether so that you know how to interact with them. Table 11-3 describes in depth the mobs you should know, where to find them, and what their behavior is.

TABLE 11-3 **The Nether's Mobs**

Mob Name	Where You Can Find It	Behavior
Zombified piglin	Nether Wastes, Crimson Forest, nether fortress	These mobs are not hostile unless you attack them. When you do attack a zombified piglin, all zombified piglins within a large radius attack you until approximately 30 seconds have passed. Oh, and the timer resets if you attack again!
Piglin	Nether Wastes, Crimson Forest, bastion remnant	Piglins are also neutral mobs. They aren't aggressive if you're wearing any pieces of gold armor. Even while you're wearing a piece of gold armor, piglins can attack you if you open a chest near them. They can also break any kind of gold near them, or attack other piglins or piglin brutes. Piglins are also lured by gold, similar to animals, using their favorite food.
Piglin brute	Bastion remnant	Unlike other piglins, piglin brutes attack you without cause, making them hostile. Piglin brutes spawn only in bastion remnants, so you can easily avoid them, if you want. Piglin brutes also inflict significantly more damage than a normal piglin. This type of piglin is all business and exists only to kill you.

Mob Name	Where You Can Find It	Behavior
Hoglin	Crimson Forest, bastion remnant	Hoglins are the pigs of the Nether. Hoglins even drop porkchops! These Nether animals are dangerous and inflict a lot of damage. When hoglins hit you, they also fling you into the air, inflicting more fall damage after you land. As with piglins and zombified piglins, if you attack a hoglin, all other hoglins around you start attacking you.
Ghast	Nether Wastes, Soul Sand Valley, Basalt Deltas	A *ghast* is a large flying creature that shoots fireballs out of its mouth. Ghast fireballs, when they're landing, destroy the area that the fireballs strike and can inflict as much as 25 damage points, depending on the difficulty. Their fireballs also can be hit and redirected if you time your defense well. Ghasts are hard to kill, so bring a bow and some arrows so that you're fully prepared!
Blaze	Nether fortress	When attacking, blaze fly and shoot 3 small fireballs at a time. These fireballs do damage and light the ground on fire. A blaze's fireballs are far less deadly than a ghast's. Blazes can be hurt by snowballs — this is a surprisingly effective way to kill them. A shield can block all attacks made by blaze.
Wither skeleton	Nether fortress	Wither skeletons wander around the nether fortress aimlessly until locking on to a player. If you get hit by a wither skeleton, it not only inflicts as much as 12 damage but also gives you the wither effect, which deals 1 damage every 2 seconds. Wither skeletons run away from wolves, similarly to normal skeletons.
Strider	Lava sea, delta, and all biomes	Striders spawn on lava and walk around on lava. If these mobs walk on land, they get cold and start walking slowly. You can put a saddle on one and ride it, but you can move a strider only by crafting a warped fungus on a stick, which combines a fishing rod and a warped fungus.

(continued)

TABLE 11-3 *(continued)*

Mob Name	Where You Can Find It	Behavior
Magma cube	Nether Wastes, Basalt Deltas, nether fortress, bastion remnant	Magma cubes are the nether version of slimes in the Overworld. When killed, they multiply and become weaker and smaller until their smallest version, which can be killed with no weapon in a single hit. Magma cubes drop magma cream, and — unlike slimes — the smallest version of them can deal damage to you.

TIP

Mobs in the Nether are fast and sometimes cannot be outrun or else they easily corner you. Building barricades with blocks might be handy if you need to heal.

Bartering with piglins

Piglins are attracted to gold and follow you if you hold a gold ingot in your hand. These mobs also barter items for gold with you.

Simply find a piglin and drop a gold ingot on the ground for them to pick up. They will run toward the gold ingot and then pick up the gold and examine it. After 6 to 8 seconds of examination, they take the gold and give you an item in return.

These are the most notable items that piglins can drop:

>> Enchanted book with soul speed (varying levels)

>> Iron boots with soul speed (varying levels)

>> Arrows (in Java Edition, spectral arrows)

>> Nether quarts (5–12)

>> Potion of fire resistance

>> Ender pearls (2–4)

Exploring the nether structures

The main reason for going to the Nether is to find a nether fortress and collect blaze powder. We talk more about this topic in the section "Grabbing resources before leaving the Nether," later in this chapter. The next several sections describe several other structures in the Nether that are worth visiting in order to build up your Minecraft arsenal.

Navigating the nether fortress

The nether fortress, shown in Figure 11-2, is a fortress composed of nether brick, which is a dark, redstone-like block. The nether fortress is dangerous, but necessary to visit to reach The End dimension. The main reason you should journey to a nether fortress is for blaze mobs, who drop blaze rods, which in turn can be crafted into blaze powder.

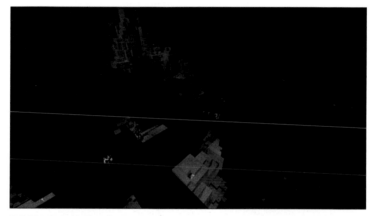

FIGURE 11-2: Nether fortress.

The nether fortress contains both indoor and outdoor areas. The indoor areas are corridors that can contain chests and other rooms. The most notable room is one that contains stairs leading to the exterior areas. To the left and right of the stairs is nether wart, a plant-like block that is vital for creating potions.

REMEMBER

Nether wart is found in both of the nether structures listed in this section, but the nether wart resource is easier to obtain in a nether fortress, and only in the specific room in the nether fortress with the stairs. Grab some nether wart whenever you see it so that you can grow more when you're back in the Overworld. Also, be sure to grab soul sand if you see it in the Nether, because soul sand is the only block that nether wart can grow on.

The exterior of the nether fortress is where you can find blaze spawners. This is one way of finding blaze in a nether fortress and is, arguably, the easiest way to find blaze. A blaze spawner is always in a little cage-like structure.

Blaze mobs can also spawn in areas that are in complete darkness in a nether fortress. You can make a farm for blaze mobs in either light or darkness, but a blaze spawner guarantees that only blaze mobs will spawn. Normally, if you clear a dark area for a blaze farm without a blaze spawner, blaze mobs spawn, but all other mobs that naturally spawn in the nether fortress also spawn in that area.

The exterior of the nether fortress also contains long walkways filled with mobs. This is where wither skeletons spawn, along with normal skeletons and a few other mobs. Wither skeletons come in groups of five, so make sure you can take on all five at one time.

TIP

One thing we do in sticky situations is create a line of blocks at head height, leaving everything below open so that we can attack the mob's feet, although they can't reach us.

Tiptoeing through a bastion remnant

Bastion remnants, informally known as *bastions,* are large, black structures that contain treasure, chests with loot, and lots and lots of piglin mobs. Of all the piglin mobs, it's arguably much harder to traverse and survive in a bastion remnant than in the rest of the Nether. Minecraft has four types of bastion remnants:

>> **Housing units:** Housing unit remnants have two buildings that surround a courtyard. The buildings contain house-like structures with chests and, often, blocks of gold. The middle of the courtyard features nether wart and, often, a chest. Housing unit remnants are another way to obtain nether wart.

>> **Hoglin stables:** Hoglin stable remnants contain 3 large, foundational structures — and one of those structures has 12 gold blocks on top. Broken hoglin stable remnants are on either side of the main bastion, which is littered with hoglin and piglin mobs. Not a lot of chests have loot in a hoglin stable remnant, but there are some chests in these structures. Neither do they contain a lot of gold blocks, aside from the 12 on the pillar.

- **>> Bridge:** A broken-up bridge leads into the bridge remnant, with a slightly misshapen piglin face as the entrance. The broken-up bridge comes out of the piglin's mouth. On the edge of the bridge is a stack of 16 gold blocks. After you're inside from the bridge, you can see that the remnant contains multiple walkways. A bridge remnant has no chests with loot, but there are more gold blocks to find.

- **>> Treasure:** Treasure remnants are the jackpot of all the bastion remnants. Treasure remnants contain a large structure that has a bridge leading to an actual treasure room, as shown in Figure 11-3. Underneath that bridge are lava basins, so watch out! In the treasure room are multiple bridges that lead to heaps of gold and possibly a chest with loot. Under the bridge, you can find a lava basin with a magma cube spawner. The treasure itself is usually guarded by only one or two piglin mobs, so accessing it should be easier than accessing most of the other rooms.

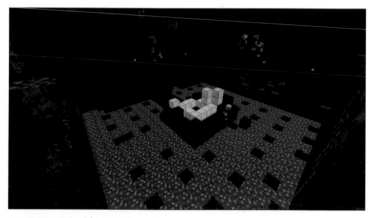

FIGURE 11-3: Inside a treasure room.

Because different types of bastion remnants can lead to different results, it's good to know what type of remnant you're entering. You aren't required to visit a bastion remnant, but if you're able to get some loot or gold blocks, it might be worth your time.

The loot in bastion remnant chests is more valuable than most chests in the Overworld. Specifically, chests in a treasure remnant can contain enchanted diamond armor and swords and regular diamond armor. The other bastion remnant types also contain impressive items, like gold, iron, gold tools and armor, diamond tools, enchanted crossbows, golden apples, and ancient debris and netherite scraps. To find out more about enchantments and powering up, see Chapter 10.

WARNING

Piglin mobs become hostile if you access a chest near them or destroy any kind of gold. If you peek through a piglin's chest or go salvage its gold blocks, you might be greeted by an angry piglin wanting your death. Make sure you plan your escape route before you go collect treasure.

Converting a ruined portal into a working portal

If you find yourself lost in the Nether and not knowing where your portal went, look no further, because there are ruined portals in the Nether as well! To turn a ruined portal into a working portal, look for obsidian to finish the ruined portal in either the chest near the ruined portal, by bartering with piglin mobs, or in other chests scattered throughout the bastion remnants and the nether fortress.

Ruined portals work and generate in almost exactly the same way in both the Nether and the Overworld. Sometimes, you can find a block of gold on top. Grab some loot and get out of there!

Advancing in the Nether

You can leave the Nether whenever you want. There is no shame in realizing that you aren't powerful enough or ready to go through the Nether. So here are some of the ways we like to keep ourselves safe in the Nether:

>> **Bridge safely.** A building technique called *bridging* is a necessity in surviving the Nether whenever you need to pass through large gaps of land with lava between them, or to reach a nether fortress across from a lava lake. To bridge safely, hold the Crouch button while you slowly move backward, toward a ledge. Place blocks behind you so that you continue to move backward, toward your destination.

Don't let go of the crouch, or else when you reach the edge, you'll just walk off. Also, if you hear a mob — specifically, a ghast — watch for fireballs! You don't want to get knocked off the bridge. Create a handrail on the bridge, if needed, so that fireballs hit the handrail before reaching you.

>> **Run for cover.** When you get into an altercation with a mob that you don't think you can win, make like Brandon Flowers from the rock band The Killers and, as his hit song, says, run for cover! To avoid mobs, create a hole to run into, and place blocks behind you so that mobs cannot come in. Then, after healing, break the bottom blocks so that you can attack the mob's legs and they can't attack you.

>> **Out of food — hoglins drop porkchops!** If you find yourself out of food in the Nether, building a hoglin farm for food is your best bet. Hoglin mobs are scary and can do a lot of damage, but if you strategize successfully, you can create a delicious meal with the hoglin mobs you encounter. If you manage to catch hoglin mobs on fire when they die, they will drop cooked porkchops — no furnace or smoker necessary!

REMEMBER

Normal piglin mobs start attacking you only if you either attack one of them first or you aren't wearing any gold armor. Before you go into the Nether, make sure you find or make some gold armor. Also, be cautious when mining gold. If you're too close to a piglin while mining gold, they will start attacking you.

Grabbing resources before leaving the Nether

If you're coming to the Nether with the intent of gaining the necessary items to find and defeat the ender dragon, these are the resources you need:

>> **Blaze powder:** Blaze powder combined with ender pearls creates eyes of ender, which is how you both find and activate the portal to The End. Grab 12–16 blaze powder, at minimum, to make eyes of ender. See the section "Adventuring to The End" for more details. Blaze powder is also useful for creating potions — specifically, potions of strength — which can be handy in your fight against the ender dragon.

>> **Ender pearls:** Ender pearls are not needed in order to be collected here, but they are much easier to obtain in the Nether. We suggest collecting 12–16 ender pearls before leaving. The easiest method is to barter with piglins and get the 4.7% chance that they drop ender pearls. Another way is using the Warped Forest biome to your advantage. You may recall that only endermen can spawn in the Warped Forest biome, making it a helpful place to farm ender pearls naturally.

>> **Nether wart:** Nether wart is another crucial ingredient in potion making. Nether wart can only be found in the Nether and should be obtained when leaving the Nether. If you get a nether wart, you can always grow more of it with some soul sand.

>> **Soul sand and magma blocks:** Soul sand, which is useful for base-making, is used to grow nether wart. Magma blocks can be used in mob farms and are a good way to defend a base. When placed underneath water source blocks, magma blocks suck down water and anything else occupying that space downward and soul sand upward. This is useful for creating water elevators in the Overworld.

Killing blaze mobs can be difficult and sometimes tedious. To kill blaze mobs effectively, bar off the blaze spawner area. When you block off this area, no other mobs can come and bother you. Bring a shield to block hits made by blaze mobs. Attack the blaze mobs with your sword, axe, or even snowballs. Snowballs can deal 3 damage to blaze mobs, so you need 7 snowballs to kill a blaze. If you want a solid, ranged weapon to kill blaze mobs, snowballs aren't a bad option. Figure 11-4 shows off one of our blaze killing machines.

Leaving the Nether

You can leave the Nether in two ways: die or exit through a portal. The best option is to remember your way back to the portal from which you originally entered, but if you aren't that lucky, try to bring extra resources with you to create another portal. You can also find a ruined portal, as we describe earlier in this chapter.

Leaving the Nether takes you back to the Overworld using the same coordinates as the Nether but with an 8x multiplier on the x and z coordinates. So, every block you move in the Nether is 8 blocks moved in the Overworld.

FIGURE 11-4: Blaze killing machine.

You spawn in either a newly generated portal in the Overworld or a portal that's relatively close to the coordinates you're transported to. The nether portal you came from and the Overworld portal close to the coordinates you were transported to are connected, and you're routed through the existing portal in the Overworld.

TIP

Because of these properties of linking portals in the Nether, we like to create a highway in the Nether that takes us to a portal that's connected to a place somewhere in the Overworld. We usually create one for our main base, one for a farm, and one for a specific biome, for example. These highway systems from the Nether to the Overworld are more efficient than highway systems from the Overworld to the Nether because of the 8x multiplier to your coordinates, as mentioned earlier.

Adventuring to The End

After you have collected ender pearls and blaze powder from the Nether, you're almost ready to conquer the ultimate challenge in Minecraft: Find The End and defeat the ender dragon!

Your first task with the materials you gathered from The End is to craft eyes of ender, which look like ender pearls but with an iris and pupil on each block. (If you're familiar with the *Lord of the Rings* trilogy, they look like a blueish green version of Eye of Sauron.) You can throw eyes of ender as though they're ender pearls, except that eyes of ender always travel in the same direction, toward the Stronghold.

Bringing along items to help find The End

Before going to the Stronghold and fighting the ender dragon, make sure you're prepared. Before you leave, pack these items to bring along:

>> **Armor, preferably diamond but iron for the determined:** Before going off and defeating the ender dragon, you need to be able to absorb some damage. If you're confident in your ability to heal, or confident in not getting hurt, bring iron armor.

>> **Melee weapons, both an axe and a sword:** The ender dragon can take physical damage when perching on the exit portal, so it's important to bring both an axe and a sword. Axes deal more damage and affect the dragon more than a sword.

>> **Projectile weapons, bow or crossbow, arrows, and snowballs:** The ender dragon flies around, so if you want to hit it from afar, you need to throw projectiles at it. The ender dragon also gets healed by end crystals, which can be destroyed by any projectile (even snowballs). We describe strategies to defeat the ender dragon later in this chapter, in the section "Fighting the ender dragon."

>> **A bed:** Before you leave for The End, you should know that, because of its difficulty, you're likely to die there. Bringing a bed to set your spawn point in the portal room is a useful way to make sure you return directly to the location from which you want to try again. This way, you can get right back in the fight without needing to travel there again and start over!

>> **Food, both healing and saturating:** You most likely need to heal at some point during your fight with the ender dragon, or journey to the Stronghold. Regular cooked foods will do the job, but if you come across either a golden apple or an enchanted golden apple in your journey, collect them because you'll need all the nutrition you can get in your fight with the ender dragon.

>> **A pickaxe:** To get into the Stronghold, you need to mine downward. After you're in The End, you'll likely also need to mine your way out of where you spawned. Bring a pickaxe to make both tasks possible.

>> **Potions:** After you have been to the Nether, you're magical — you can craft potions! To learn how to make potions, see Chapter 10. We suggest bringing along a potion of strength and regeneration for your journey to The End. A splash potion of instant health is also useful.

>> **Water bucket:** Water buckets can be used to break your fall by placing water beneath you before you hit the ground. The ender dragon has a tendency to send you into the air to fall to your death, so water buckets can be useful in preventing this type of demise. Also, any endermen you encounter in your battle are allergic to water and cannot step in it.

>> **Miscellaneous, such as torches, building blocks, and wood:** It's always good to have the basic survival items on you when you go out exploring. The Stronghold is a dark area, so being able to light it with torches is helpful for seeing in the dark. In The End, building blocks might be useful to get to the main island or to build up to a pillar. Wood is always good for making sticks and other tools, and for other general uses. Bring anything else that you think might be useful. If you truly enjoy using a compass, bring one along!

Locating the Stronghold

The Stronghold is the structure that holds the portal to The End. Throwing an eye of ender always leads you toward the Stronghold because it always moves in its direction. If you're close enough, your eye of ender will go into the ground, showing that you're on top of the Stronghold.

After you throw an eye of ender, it has a 20 percent chance of breaking, rather than falling for you to pick up. Keeping an extra eye of ender may come in handy in the event the first one breaks.

To reach the Stronghold, follow the direction the eye went when thrown and it eventually brings you to the Stronghold. The Stronghold is normally just a couple hundred blocks from where you first threw the eye of ender.

When the eye of ender moves downward after you throw it, you know that you're on top of the Stronghold and can dig straight down into it. If you're lucky, you can sometimes find one sticking right out of the ocean, but those are *rare.*

Exploring the Stronghold

After you have entered the Stronghold, it's time to explore. The Stronghold contains a lot of loot and unique rooms to explore. The ultimate goal is to find the portal room inside the Stronghold. Table 11-4 describes the various rooms you can find in the Stronghold and details the items you can find in them.

TABLE 11-4 Stronghold Rooms

Room Type	Description
Staircase	Can be either a straight staircase or a spiraling staircase. Either one can lead to a dead end, but often leads to a lower floor or an upper floor.
Corridor	A hallway that leads to more rooms (yes, self-explanatory), and sometimes contains a dead end. The most useful corridors contain a chest in the middle.
Empty prison cells	Sometimes containing iron doors, a cell made up of iron bars. Nothing spawns in it.
Large rooms	A larger room with multiple exits, sometimes containing a small centerpiece.
Libraries	Can spawn with 1 or 2 floors. It has bookshelves and oak planks and fences dispersed throughout, and also contains cobwebs and 1 chest with loot per floor.
End portal room	Contains the portal that you can activate to go to The End, and with some lava- and silverfish-infested blocks.

REMEMBER

The Stronghold isn't terribly dangerous, but it does naturally spawn mobs that you find underground. Be wary, but if you're prepared to fight the ender dragon, you shouldn't need to be worried about fighting the mobs that appear in the Stronghold.

The foreboding portal room

Congratulations — you made it to the end portal! This room contains a staircase leading up to the portal frame. You will see 12 frames surrounding a 3x3 square. Lava flows underneath it and in the corners of the room.

First, to make sure no mobs follow you into the room, place blocks barricading the entry. Now is the time to find a place to put your bed and add a chest to store any items you don't want to take with you. Interact with the bed to set your respawn location. This becomes helpful if you end up dying in The End and want to continue the fight.

The portal room contains a silverfish spawner. You can place torches all around the spawner if you want to preserve the spawner while not letting it spawn silverfish. Or, you can break the spawner if you never want to spawn silverfish.

TIP

Silverfish don't drop anything, so we believe that farming them is a waste of time — we always break the spawner.

The portal room also contains silverfish-infested blocks. If you get close enough to break a silverfish-infested block, the block disappears and a silverfish comes out, trying to kill you! Silverfish don't have a lot of health and don't deal a lot of damage, but they're fast and small, so you should kill them as soon as you see them. A decent sword can kill one in a single hit.

The portal is in the middle of the room. It spawns, on occasion, with eyes of ender prefilled in some spots. There is a 1 in a trillion chance of all empty slots being filled entirely with eyes of ender, so you should have enough eyes of ender to fill the rest of the slots. You may need to fill all of them if none is filled in. Interact with an empty portal frame with an eye of ender in your hand to place it in an empty slot. You cannot remove it afterward, but this is the main use for eyes of ender, so don't worry about using it this way.

After the portal is filled, you hear a sudden and loud boom along with the portal activating. Revel in your achievement and the feeling of pride/anxiety. Figure 11-5 shows off an activated portal.

Ending with The End

If you remember the portal from the section "The foreboding portal room," all you need to do is walk into it to be teleported instantly to The End. The nether portal gives you time to think, allowing you to step out of the portal if you don't want to go. If you touch the end portal, however, you're teleported instantly.

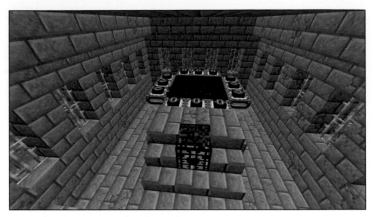

FIGURE 11-5: An activated end portal.

Entering The End

When you arrive in The End, spawn a 3x3 area of obsidian in the area you arrive in, with a 3x3x3 space above it containing air. This way, you won't suffocate if you spawn inside the island.

You might spawn outside of the island and have to bridge your way to the main island. You might also spawn inside the island (under the ground) and have to mine a staircase up to the top of the island.

When first entering The End, you see one main island with large obsidian towers topped with crystals. These end crystals can sometimes be surrounded by iron bars. The end crystals have a beam shooting toward the ender dragon, and healing it.

Notice also an altar made out of bedrock in the middle of the island. This altar is your exit portal after you defeat the ender dragon.

TIP

Keep your head low in The End. Lots and lots of endermen await you here! They are one of two mobs that can spawn naturally in The End, so you don't want to accidentally aggravate one by looking directly into its eyes!

Fighting the ender dragon

Fighting the ender dragon is the toughest melee battle you face in the game for a while. You have lots of technical skills to consider while fighting an ender dragon, as we describe in the next few sections.

Breaking the crystals

The first step in defeating the ender dragon is to destroy the end crystals that lie atop the obsidian pillars. The ender dragon heals all damage dealt to it if you don't destroy these crystals first.

Minecraft has two types of these obsidian pillars: one with the crystal open on top and another where the crystal is enclosed in a cage.

The crystals can be destroyed when any projectile hits the crystal, or if you punch it with something. If the crystal is healing the dragon when it gets destroyed, it will do damage to the dragon. Make sure you practice your aim as seen in Figure 11-6! If you have a bow, use it with the infinity enchantment (mentioned in Chapter 10) so that you don't have to bring a lot of arrows (see Figure 11-6). For the crystals that are not in cages, you can just shoot at them with an arrow or even snowballs!

FIGURE 11-6: Firing arrows at the crystal.

To find the crystals that are in cages, look for a small opening in the corners. Try to aim your projectile *just* right, but keep in mind that it's a *difficult* shot. We suggest building a staircase up to the pillar until you reach the last block so that only your head can reach the crystal.

End crystals deal up to 72 damage, so if you punch the crystal, make sure your feet aren't on the same block level as a crystal. Try to be 1 block lower. Or move close enough to shoot the crystal, but not enough to take damage.

Defeating the dragon

After you have taken down all the end crystals, it's time to start hurting the ender dragon. You can deal damage to the ender dragon in two ways: Attack it with a projectile, such as shooting it with a bow, or try a melee attack, if it gets close enough to hit.

The dragon often *perches* on top of the middle bedrock structure. You can tell that the dragon is about to perch when it starts making small circles around the middle of the island. When this happens, run into the bedrock structure and stay there until it perches.

Do *not* jump while you're in the bedrock structure and the ender dragon is perched. If you jump, the ender dragon can fling you far up in the air, ensuring that you die from fall damage. Instead, you can deal the maximum amount of damage to its head, which is the most vulnerable spot. Use an axe or a sword to continually attack the head until enough damage is done to kill the dragon or the dragon flies away.

Repeat this process, but also shoot it from afar while it's away.

The dragon can breathe dragon's breath on the ground, causing you damage if you stand in it. Try to avoid damage if you can't run away from the dragon's breath.

Benefitting from some outstanding tips and tricks

Here are some of our best tips for defeating and surviving the ender dragon fight:

>> **Use the water bucket you brought to keep endermen away.** Endermen cannot walk in water. If you accidentally anger a bunch of them, place some water so that they cannot get near you.

>> **Use the water bucket to save your fall.** When you land in water, all fall damage is negated. When falling, place water preemptively and aim for the water after being flung into the

air, or after being flung into the air before you hit the ground. If you time it well, you can place the water right where you're about to land and save your fall.

>> **Eat a golden apple, or an enchanted one.** If you have been saving your golden apples, now is the time to use them! An enchanted golden apple gives you insane regeneration powers briefly, and resistance, allowing you to take more damage. Eating a golden apple is a good way to acquire regeneration powers and some extra hearts.

>> **Use those potions!** Potions are your best friends in this fight. Strength is overpowered, and at a second level makes you deal 260 percent more damage! Regeneration potions and instant health potions are helpful, too.

Entering The End via the exit portal

After the ender dragon takes its last hit, it freezes and starts to deteriorate into a bright flash. The ender dragon drops tons of experience points (xp) and, when fully gone, spawns the exit portal inside the bedrock structure. A dragon egg also spawns on top of the structure.

When you step into the exit portal, you see the game's credits and you return to your spawn point. This is a good time to reflect on all the cool things you did — congratulations! This isn't the true end of Minecraft, however — it only gets better from here, and there is much more you can do.

Going Beyond the Ender Dragon

After the ender dragon has been defeated, end gateways show up. These little bedrock structures have a portal in the middle. If you enter the portal by crawling with water or using an ender pearl to get inside, you're teleported to the outer end islands, near a connected gate.

REMEMBER

The only way to get back from The End alive is to go through the exit portal in the middle of the main island. Remember where your end gateways are so that you don't get lost and you can find your way back.

Now that you're on the outer islands of The End, you can go exploring to find structures. A bunch of small islands have chorus fruit on them — a fruit that, when eaten, teleports you a random location within 8 blocks in any direction.

Minecraft also has End Cities (as seen in Figure 11-7). A small city contains a few large, tower-like buildings. Each tower contains 5 different rooms. Most of these towers contain empty rooms, but some have *banner rooms*, identified by the banners hanging on the walls, and some of these have a shulker mob hidden near the top of the room.

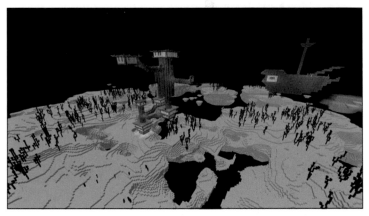

FIGURE 11-7: The End City.

The shulker mob is exclusive to The End. Shulkers are hidden in boxes, and they shoot you with a tracking blob that, when it hits, deals the levitation effect. The levitation effect causes you to float if it's active. If a shulker hits you repeatedly, the levitation timer increases, causing you to float longer. A shulker drops shulker shells, which can be used to craft *shulker boxes,* a storage block that carries items even when they're broken or in your inventory.

The other notable room in an End City is the *loot room,* containing two chests with *valuable* loot. These chests often have diamonds, high-level enchanted diamond armor, high-level enchanted diamond tools, mending enchantment books, and much more.

One other building, which has a lower chance of spawning in an End City, is an *end ship.* To determine whether an end ship has spawned, look for a floating ship in the sky with an ender dragon head at the front.

If you find an end ship, be aware that three shulkers spawn on top of each end ship to guard it — either evade them and run to the interior of the ship or try to fight the shulkers.

The interior of the end ship contains a brewing stand that has instant health II potions (see Chapter 10) inside. Further inside the end ship is a treasure room, which is guarded by another shulker. The treasure room contains two loot chests, with very valuable loot, and, more importantly, an elytra in the item frame between them.

Elytra are wings that allow you to glide. Place elytra in your chest plate armor to activate the gliding ability. To glide once in your chest plate armor, hold down the Jump button while you're in the air. It might take some time to get used to gliding, but it's fun when you're able to do it!

If you're going fast enough on an elytra and hit a wall, it deals damage to you. It also deals fall damage if you land with too much speed going downward.

Surviving the Afterglow of The End

The End feels like the last part of the game, but Minecraft has a lot more to do! You can build out your base. You can become as strong as you possibly can. You can build more farms and automate everything. The list goes on and on.

One of the first things you should do after defeating the ender dragon is defeat the wither, a boss that can be either easy or difficult to defeat, depending on your skill level. The wither is spawned by creating a T shape with soul sand and placing three wither skeleton skulls on top of it.

After spawning, the wither starts to charge up. The wither cannot be damaged during this phase, and when fully charged, it creates a small explosion. Once charged, the wither attacks you and other nearby mobs with small explosives that look like wither skeleton skulls. Block these with your shield.

During the first half of the wither's health range, shoot arrows and other projectiles at it and try to stay alive! Run and heal, if you must. After the first half of the wither's health level is depleted, a small barrier appears around the wither, preventing projectiles from having any effect in killing the wither.

During the second half of the wither's health, melee is your only way to damage the wither. When you have a high damage-dealing sword or axe, however, defeating the wither should be a piece of cake. Be cautious and heal, if necessary, like you did in the first half of the health level.

After killing the wither, the now dead wither drops a nether star, which is used to craft a beacon, as detailed in the next section.

Building the Beacon

One of the most powerful items in Minecraft is the beacon. It can be created only after defeating the wither, which yields a *nether star*. To make a beacon (see Figure 11-8), you need these items:

>> 3 obsidian

>> 5 glass

>> 1 nether star

FIGURE 11-8: Setting up a beacon.

After placing the beacon on the ground, make a solid pyramid of metal blocks (blocks of iron, gold, diamond, netherite, or emerald) beneath the beacon. The simplest pyramid you can create for this task is a single 3x3 square.

When you finish, the beacon automatically sends a light beam into the sky. The beam is white unless you place stained glass in the path of the beam, which changes the beam to the color of the glass. The larger the pyramid, the greater the power of the beacon. The largest pyramid is built from 164 blocks with a 9x9 layer on the bottom, a 7x7 layer next, a 5x5 later after that one, and then a 3x3 layer on top. However, unless you're playing in Creative mode, it's nearly impossible to find enough gold, diamond, or emeralds to create the largest pyramid.

The cheapest way to build a beacon is by using iron blocks, but you can use gold, diamond, or emerald if you're feeling artistic. At the time of this writing, you gain no advantage by using more powerful minerals. Minerals can be mixed to create the pyramid. Players with vast resources often create pyramids by using an alternating pattern, for added aesthetics.

The purpose of the high-end and powerful beacon is to provide bonus powers to all nearby players. For example, a beacon might allow all players within a radius to run faster or absorb less damage.

To make the beacon work, right-click the beacon to open the Beacon menu. Five primary power icons and one secondary power icon appear. You can select only one primary power and one secondary power, and you can select a power only if you have built a large enough pyramid beneath the beacon.

The required size of the pyramid is shown in the image next to each icon and described in Table 11-5. The icons and powers on the Beacon menu are also explained in the table.

After you have selected a primary power (and a secondary power, if the pyramid is large enough), place an iron ingot, a gold ingot, a diamond, a netherite ingot, or an emerald in the slot provided and click the green check mark. The beacon constantly powers you as long as you're in its range (from 20 to 50 blocks, depending on the size of the pyramid). If you want to switch powers, a new gem (iron or diamond, for example) must be fed into the beacon using the GUI.

TABLE 11-5 Beacon Icons and Powers

Icon	Name	Ability	Pyramid Level
	Speed	Increased movement	Level 1
	Haste	Increased mining speed	Level 1
	Resistance	Increased armor rating	Level 2
	Jump Boost	Increased jump height and distance	Level 2
	Strength	Increased melee damage	Level 3
	Regeneration	Regenerated heart health	Level 4 and can be combined with any one other power

TIP

If you want the beacon to rest on the ground, build your pyramid underground.

Beacons require an unobstructed view of the sky above them (or they can have transparent blocks above beacons). The beacon beam fades as it reaches higher into the sky and is practically invisible in the Nether. More commonly, a beacon beam is strong enough to create a large landmark and is highly visible.

Chapter **12**

Expanding Your Minecraft Experience

M inecraft doesn't have to be just a survival experience in SinglePlayer mode: You can play with friends in Survival mode or with friends on custom public servers. Public servers often have a SinglePlayer version of Minecraft as well, but it's more fun to play with a friend.

Starting and Joining a Private Multiplayer World

Minecraft is fantastic to play on your own, but persuading a friend, partner, or family member to play with you makes for a rewarding experience. There are different ways to play locally, depending on which version you play. The following sections describe both the *Minecraft Java Edition* and *Minecraft Bedrock Edition* ways of joining a local world.

Bedrock Edition

In Bedrock Edition, you must be friends on your Microsoft account with the person you want to play with. A quick search online for how to add a friend in Minecraft leads you to instructions showing you how to add a friend on your particular gaming console.

To play with friends on a PC when you're creating your world, make sure you toggle the Multiplayer Game option after choosing Edit Settings ⇨ Multiplayer.

Once the world has been created, follow these steps to invite your friends on a PC:

1. **Open the menu and click the Invite to Game button, as shown in Figure 12-1.**

2. **Select the friend or friends you want to invite to your game, and then click the Send Invite button.**

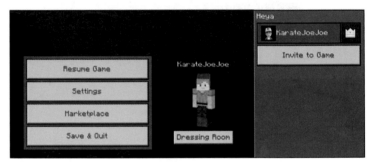

FIGURE 12-1: Inviting a player to the game in Bedrock Edition.

When your friend accepts the invite, they're automatically added to the game. From there, you can continue the game with that person.

When you're playing with friends on a local world, the world is open to you and your friends only while the creator of the world is playing it. When the person who created the world logs off, no one else can play in the world until logging back on and reinviting all the players.

Java Edition

Minecraft Java Edition doesn't easily work with friends, but it's possible. If you play with someone who uses the same Wi-Fi connection, you can start playing in a *LAN world,* which is a multiplayer server connected through the router.

Once you have started a singleplayer Minecraft world, open the game's menu by pressing Esc and following these steps:

1. **Click the Open to LAN button.**

   After clicking said button, you can select the settings (shown in Figure 12-2) that apply for all players who join the world.

2. **Click the Start LAN World button.**

   You see a prompt asking you to allow the necessary port to be opened. Accept the prompt and then enjoy!

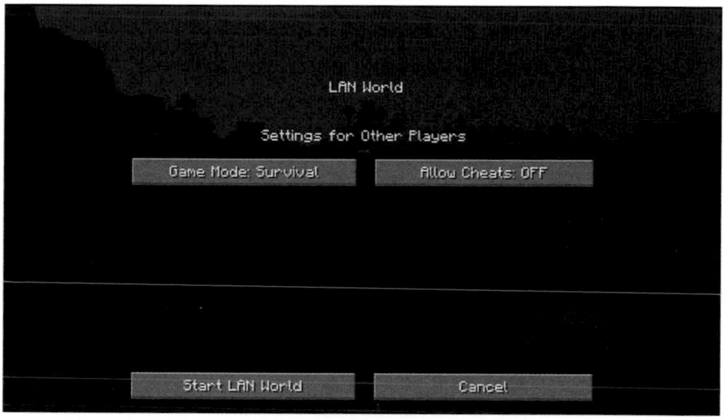

FIGURE 12-2: Java Edition LAN world settings screen.

From here, whenever the world is closed on your computer, just as in Bedrock Edition, the world closes for all players.

If you want to join someone who has started a LAN world, click the Multiplayer button on the main menu. After the LAN world is started, it shows up in the area labeled Scanning for Games On Your Local Network.

Creating a Realms world

Minecraft offers a service called Minecraft Realms in both editions. It's a way to run a Minecraft world without a designated host. A subscription to it can cost as much as $8 per month.

Minecraft Realms is a useful way to create an online world if you lack the correct components or knowledge to start a Minecraft server that can handle lots of players at a time.

Once you buy the subscription to a Realms world, in both editions of Minecraft, just edit and create the world under its designated tab.

Joining Public Servers

You can join private servers in Minecraft, but if you want to play custom minigames, custom worlds, or custom universes, an online server such as Hypixelmight be for you.

Though public servers can be dangerous and filled with people who use harsh language, all the servers we mention are safe and have good moderation teams to prevent mean-spirited people from playing. If you decide to find other public servers, however, be wary of other players. Chapter 13 also addresses the dangers of online play.

TIP

If you're a parental figure to a young child, be wary whenever you're watching what your child does in Minecraft. Though we're unaware of Minecraft-related crime statistics (we don't work for the FBI, after all), this is prime territory for potential predators and bad influences on children. Encourage your children to stick to the servers mentioned in this book or (if you have some experience with the game) those you're already familiar with.

Bedrock Edition

After clicking the Play button, rather than click the Create New button (as you may have in the past, if you play on single player worlds), click the Servers tab to see recommended servers that are safe to join and play on. The Hive is our go-to choice.

Join a server and start playing!

REMEMBER

These servers are safe for having fun alone or with friends. Some servers are even dedicated to different skills that can make you better at playing the game.

If you want to join a custom server that you find online, look at the bottom of the servers list for the Add Server button. Click it and enter the following information:

>> **Server name:** Enter whatever name you want. Most people set it to whatever name the server already has, but the choice is up to you.

>> **Server address:** The game uses this URL to find the server, so leave this one as the default text. For example, the Hive's North American server address is `http://ca.hivebedrock.network`.

>> **Port:** Leave this one as the default, 19132, unless otherwise specified by the server. Make sure that this port number is open on your computer and network so that you can access the server.

Java Edition

Java Edition has lots of similarities with Bedrock Edition when entering an online multiplayer server. Click the Multiplayer button and allow any necessary connections that your operating system needs. Then click either the Direct Connection button or the Add Server button.

From here, you can add a server using the server's address. A *server address* is a URL that the server owners own and maintain, so if you don't have one, don't worry about this part. You can find lists of specific servers online by searching online for a specific minigame or type.

TIP

Our favorite server, a hugely popular Minecraft server, is `http://hypixel.net`, which features our favorite custom gamemode, Skyblock. In the Skyblock gamemode, you start on a small island with nothing but a tree. Hypixel's version of Skyblock features many challenges and custom items that aren't in vanilla Minecraft made specific by the gamemode's creators.

When you're adding a server, you see a button that lets you determine whether resource packs on servers are enabled. A *resource pack* is a asset package that changes the game's art. For instance, a resource pack can turn a dirt block's asset into a stone block. It doesn't change the block, just the image assets. Sometimes, a resource pack makes assets more basic, and at other times it can make them uglier. An example of a resource pack is shown in Figure 12-3.

FIGURE 12-3: This resource pack makes the game look and feel more medieval.

"Cheating" for Minecraft

Minecraft normally uses the term *cheat* for commands and other types of content that allow you to do things that aren't part of the typical survival strategy. In the following sections, we describe various kinds of cheats in Minecraft.

In both local Minecraft worlds and online servers, the chat box often appears and tells you about one of your actions or achievements. If you're playing with friends online, you can use the chat box to send messages to each other.

You can also use the chat box to issue commands in Minecraft. You start by adding the forward slash (/) in front of the inputted command. A *command* is a bit of text that causes an action in the game in an unnatural way. For instance, rather than have a player collect a specific item, you can use the command */give <player> <item> <amount>* to provide it to them directly.

Using commands that any players can use

Minecraft has certain commands that any player can use at any time in the game. Most of these commands affect only the chat box and not the game directly. These are the two commands we use most often when playing with other players:

>> **/me:** This command puts whatever message you issue in the chat box, but with your in-game name in front of the message. For example, *me is eatin' a sandwich* produces this statement: "KarateJoeJoe is eatin' a sandwich," as shown in Figure 12-4.

```
× KarateJoeJoe is eatin' a sandwhich
<KarateJoeJoe>  /me is eatin' a sandwhich
```

FIGURE 12-4: I'm eatin' a sandwich.

>> **/msg:** You use this command to send a private message to someone. You can use it to secretly communicate with another player on a server without letting anyone else know. The command is useful for talking to friends about your supersecret plans to invade another player's base.

Typing commands that cheat

Normally, the default commands in Minecraft don't affect the game unnaturally. If you have cheats enabled, however, you can affect your world.

TIP

Type the command */help* into the chat menu to see a list of commands to choose from.

Here is a list of commands that we like to use in cheat-enabled worlds.

>> **/gamemode:** Switches between gamemodes. We use this command all the time to switch between Creative mode and Survival mode. Sometimes, we use this command in normal survival worlds by switching to Creative mode in a sticky situation to make sure we don't lose all our inventory.

>> **/gamerule:** Lets you change the options for interacting with your world, as described later in this chapter, in the section "Using gamerules to your advantage."

- **/give:** As described earlier in this chapter, can be used to give yourself or other players items needed to build structures or craft items. We use this command all the time. It's useful when we don't want to switch to Creative mode to grab an item we need.

- **/kill:** Can be used to automatically "kill" yourself or another player. It can be used to prank your friends or to return to your original spawn location in a creative world.

- **/tp:** Can take, or *teleport*, any player to any coordinate or to another player in the world.

- **/locate:** Can serve as useful tools in creative worlds to customize your world (or help you shoot screen shots for a book like the one you're reading now). We use this command all the time to pick out nice areas to plan structures or find rare biomes.

Using gamerules to your advantage

As described in the preceding section, the gamerule command affects all aspects of the game. The text you enter after giving the gamerule command is the rule you want your Minecraft world to follow. This often uses a true-or-false statement, as we explain in the following list — it describes some of the gamerules we use most often:

- **/gamerule keepInventory [true/false]:** Specifies whether all items in the inventory drop when you die. By default, the keepInventory gamerule is set to false, but when it's true, after dying you respawn with all items still in the inventory.

TIP

  It can be frustrating to die and lose all your items, so to keep things interesting and inspire plays to remain on a server, set keepInventory to true. We often use the keepInventory gamerule with friends on servers.

- **/gamerule doMobSpawning [true/false]:** Determines whether mobs spawn naturally in a world. Whenever we are in Creative mode and want to prevent mobs from getting in the way of projects, we set doMobSpawning to false. That way, we can control the conditions of the world related to mobs. Mobs can still spawn when you use the */summon* command or use spawn eggs.

» **/gamerule doDaylightCycle [true/false]:** Lets you deter-mine the environment you want your world to take on. We use doDaylightCycle if we have no reason to enter nighttime and we just want to work on a project without changing light levels.

» **/gamerule randomTickSpeed [number]:** Makes blocks grow fast or produce faster. There are 20 ticks per second in Minecraft, making the default number 3 (60 / 3). The lower the number, the slower the tick speed; the higher the number, the faster the tick speed. Therefore, if you use a randomTickSpeed gamerule with the number 3000, your world's plants and grass will start spreading and growing much faster than normal. randomTickSpeed controls the speed of your Minecraft world.

Checking Out External Sites and Resources

Minecraft can also be a form of entertainment outside of the game itself. You can find plenty of media and other resources to provide hours of entertainment using the Minecraft game as the founda-tion. People even create custom animations about Minecraft.

Watching Minecraft media

Watching Minecraft videos is the most common way to find and enjoy entertainment about Minecraft. For a generation of players who have grown up playing Minecraft — along with new genera-tions who are playing — it has created a diverse range of content for all ages to enjoy.

TIP

With the release of this book, we have created a YouTube channel that covers many topics in video format. If you want more of a visual aid to be able to follow along or learn more about a specific topic, check out the Minecraft For Dummies YouTube channel, at youtube.com/user/minecraftdummiesbook.

Finding Minecraft YouTube groups

One way to enjoy Minecraft content is to find Minecraft content creators on YouTube who play in groups and do things such as minigame tournaments with their group of other content creators. The most notable Minecraft YouTube group is known as The Hermitcraft — its members are known as Hermits.

Minecraft groups often focus on one game aspect that is common among members of their group, such as their locality or a task they excel at, like building. These groups sometimes take advantage of other members' strengths, and they interact with each other as the main selling point. Part of the fun of watching these groups is enjoying the dynamic between the various content creators.

Watching building-focused YouTube channels

Inside and outside of Minecraft groups, you can find content creators on YouTube who focus on the building aspect of Minecraft. These content creators create amazing structures, tutorials on how to make your buildings better, and even tutorials on making specific buildings.

Our favorite example of a building content creator on YouTube goes by Grian. Grian makes lighthearted content revolving around building items in Minecraft. As part of the Hermitcraft, he is known for his extravagant creations and tutorials about building. Grian makes huge entertainment out of building items inside Minecraft.

Viewing SMP YouTube videos

Survival MultiPlayer, or SMP, is a way to play Minecraft in Survival mode with friends in a multiplayer world. Many channels and a great deal of content revolve around this idea. After all, it's the basic Minecraft game — but with friends.

These YouTube videos of Minecraft content creators on YouTube playing with their friends makes for an entertaining experience. These content creators create stories, plots, and pranks on people in the worlds they play in, making it a fun experience to watch.

SMP videos, because they have many people in them, also show different perspectives. This way, you can view the story from your favorite character's perspective.

The largest SMP group is DreamSMP, organized by the most famous YouTuber in the group — Dream. This group created a survival multiplayer world that has a story written and produced by the content creators on YouTube within the group.

Speedrunning Minecraft

Another form of Minecraft entertainment is to watch speedruns of the game. In a *speedrun,* you try to beat a game as fast as possible. Minecraft has an intense speedrun community and content creator population.

The current most-famous YouTuber and Minecraft speedrunner is Dream, who has brought lots of people to the speedrunning side of Minecraft. Most of this player's videos revolve around beating Minecraft with a time constraint attached.

TIP

Speedrunning might turn out to be an activity you enjoy — it's another way you can play the game. If you enjoy a more competitive environment but still like to stick to the basic game, look up speedrunning videos and learn how to do it.

Digging into advanced topics with Minecraft tutorials

Minecraft tutorial videos are a helpful way to learn more about Minecraft and specific sections of Minecraft. If you want to learn about a specific task in the game, such as how to build structures, tutorials are mighty helpful.

We enjoy watching Minecraft tutorials about enchanting and farming and to learn about upcoming updates. Farms are a major part of how we play and how we like to automate our world. Tutorials also teach you about the more advanced game mechanics, like redstone. Because redstone is a more advanced topic, when you feel confident in your Minecraft skills, the YouTuber Mumbo Jumbo is a helpful resource to check out. This player explains redstone and offers tutorials for creating redstone contraptions and redstone-based farms (which we tell you more about in Chapter 7).

Listening to Minecraft music

Another way to absorb Minecraft media is to listen to its beautiful soundtrack. Minecraft has an extensive soundtrack, released on two albums, that makes entertaining background music as you're doing work throughout the day (or playing the game, of course).

Most songs on the Minecraft soundtrack revolve around a soft, open feeling on a piano or synthesizer. The sounds are designed for situations such as when you're exploring your favorite cave. As you explore, the music is designed to give you a deep feeling of openness, just as though you were there.

TIP

We use the Minecraft soundtrack to study and write, and it's appealing when you need music playing in the background while doing work, for example. The nature of the soundtrack also helps us focus, which helps us with our own easily distracted minds. Also, we don't feel any intense emotions or desires to sing along, because it's simply background music.

Our absolute favorite songs in Minecraft are described in this list:

>> **"Wet Hands,"** created by C418, primarily represents an old-style tuning of a piano. Most of the song has an arpeggio backing, keeping it consistent and easy to listen to.

>> **"Sweden"** is another Minecraft classic, but it's more mundane than "Wet Hands." "Sweden" consists mostly of chords on a piano that lead to an orchestra joining those chords. The song feels like it rises and then falls again — it's easy to just relax and listen to it.

>> **"Infinite Amethyst,"** created by Lena Raine, is a more complex song that has an open feeling, that feels like it is leading you to something bigger. The song itself gives you that feeling of exploring as you make your way through a cave and uncover an amethyst as the music grows louder and more intricate.

>> **"Otherside,"** also created by Lena Raine, is peppy and upbeat and much more distracting than if it were meant to serve as background music. You can find the "otherside" music disc in Minecraft.

The Part of Tens

Chapter **13**

Ten Things Adults Should Try in Minecraft (Adults Only!)

Adults can play Minecraft, too! In fact, we suspect that most people who read this book are probably curious adults like you who either have a child in their life who plays or who grew up around the game and now are curious to see what all the hype was about. This chapter is for you.

Grasp the Basics of the Game

You're probably excited to hit the ground running! To jump into the action, you first must register a Minecraft account. Then you can play in Demo mode or upgrade to the Premium account, which you need for the full version. After you've created a Minecraft account, you must buy and install the game. You can learn how to do all of this in Chapter 2, where we walk you through the steps to register an account and install the game.

Congratulations! You've successfully registered and installed Minecraft. Now you can play with other adults — or the children you're caring for.

Play with Your Children

Have children of your own? Or maybe you raise or care for someone else's children? Minecraft is a powerful tool for building bonds with your kids. Use it to dive in and truly play with the children in your life. Playing the game makes for an excellent bonding and teaching tool (as we show you later in this chapter) for connecting with your children. See Chapter 1 for more ideas about ways to play with your children in Minecraft.

Know Who Your Children Play With

Though Minecraft creates an excellent environment for playing with your own children and those you're responsible for, predators can take advantage of the multiplayer environments within Minecraft to prey on unsupervised children. Make sure you always know who your children are playing with in multiplayer environments, and be certain they're playing on safe servers known to monitor such activity.

Chapter 12 talks more about how to protect children in multiplayer environments and how to find these safer servers.

Stay Safe in Minecraft

We (meaning Jesse, the dad, who is writing this chapter) had many conversations with other parental figures in our lives who just don't seem to understand what this Minecraft thing is that their kids play. Though we hope that this book helps parents and adults better understand what this amazing platform for exploration and creativity can be, there's a good chance that safety is in the back of the mind of every parental figure who picks up this book.

The number-one safety tip we can offer is to get in and play with the children in your life! That's really what this book is about. If it saves a child's life because one more adult learned how to play Minecraft with their children, our mission is accomplished. But knowing whom they're talking to, teaching them not to chat with strangers, and knowing whom they're playing with is also important.

In Chapter 1, we offer some basic tips to keep your children safe — we highly recommend that you read those tips and discuss them with your children.

The Minecraft Wiki (minecraft.fandom.com/wiki) — as well as popular Minecraft websites and YouTube videos — can include links to malware that can infect your computer. We recommend also installing an antivirus program, such as Norton AntiVirus, to prevent this malware from infecting your computer.

Use Minecraft as a Teaching Tool

Minecraft is an incredible teaching tool! From basic geology principles and electronics, programming, and logic to basic physics and chemistry — or just plain old exploration and creativity — Minecraft can teach you and your children all these concepts.

In Chapter 1, we break down all the ways that Minecraft can be used as a teaching tool. Especially if you're a parental figure with children, you'll want to read that part.

Divorced with Kids? Coparent Better by Using Minecraft

Jesse, the dad who is writing this chapter, is a divorced single dad who coparents with the mother of some of the children who have helped write this book. Minecraft, even in a divorced, multi-household situation, is still a family affair in our household!

If you're a divorced parent who coparents with another parent of your shared children, there's a good chance your children aren't always at your house or the other parent's house. That's the fun part about playing multiplayer games in Minecraft — you don't have to live in the same place.

Use Minecraft to schedule time to play with your children while they're away and, if possible, encourage their coparent to do the same while the kids are with you. This is an amazing strategy to bond with your children. Check out the tips in Chapter 12 to find out about Minecraft multiplayer modes and how to get started playing remotely with other players (like your children).

TIP

Feeling overly ambitious? Set up your own server, or use the server of someone else you know, and set up servers named Dad's House and Mom's House. (Or, hey — we're all-inclusive here — name them Mom's and Mom's and Dad's and Dad's!) One parent can decorate their house along with the kids, and the other parent can decorate their house as well with the kids, mimicking the multihouse environment in a virtual world — but still giving the children a chance to go back-and-forth at their own pace, as *they* choose!

Learn about Minecraft

You can find a multitude of YouTube channels — like our official YouTube channel for this book, at www.youtube.com/channel/UC2DPNfMo19g-Fe5Qv5BbfBw, TikTok accounts, blogs, and books in print (including this one and others we've written) and online that will help you take your knowledge of Minecraft to the next level. Enjoy searching about Minecraft in your favorite search engine, or check out some of our favorite resources in Chapter 12 of this book.

See Minecraft as More than a Game

We love geeking out on this one. The truth is that Minecraft isn't just a game. Sure, you can play in Survival mode, advance to the Nether, beat the ender dragon, and amaze all your friends with news of how far you've advanced in the game. You can even join game mods and servers that allow you to keep score with challenges against other players.

But the real value of Minecraft lies in exploration. In 2022, as this book is being written, a lot of talk is happening around the concept of the metaverse. How meta it is that we mention this topic! (That was a dad joke.) Facebook rebranded itself as Meta, in fact. And yes, Minecraft itself is another form of the metaverse. You can even access it in virtual reality with a little effort.

A lot of question remains about how central the metaverse will be to the Internet of the future. One thing we can say is that Minecraft is *the* most downloaded metaverse-type environment on the Internet, and it allows the creation of worlds and environments and collaboration and connection unlike many other metaverse environments taking shape as we write this chapter. Time will tell how much Minecraft will evolve, but you may even be able to have business meetings in your own Minecraft office environment in the future. (Jesse is watching his kids cringe at this idea right now.)

Host a Server

If you really want to geek out on Minecraft and you have some technical skills (this topic is not for the faint of heart, and it's beyond the scope of this book), you can set up your own Minecraft server and invite others to join. Setting up your own Minecraft server is an excellent way to keep your world around as long as you like, because as long as the server is running, your world stays alive. And anyone who wants to create in your world also gets to keep their creations, assuming that you don't delete them down the road.

We walk you through the basics of the Minecraft server in Chapter 12, but for the most part, it's beyond the scope of this book. If you know enough to set up your own server, we're betting that you also know how to quickly search for instructions on your favorite search engine.

Teach a Class

Jesse (the dad who is writing this chapter) mentioned to one of his children's teachers that his children were writing *Minecraft Basics For Dummies,* and the teacher had a novel idea: She invited us to come teach the children in her class about Minecraft.

Because of the many ways you can use Minecraft to teach children, as mentioned earlier in this chapter and in Chapter 1, after you feel that you have a good grasp on the value of Minecraft, you might pick up an extra copy or two of this book and make a presentation in your own children's classroom. Reach out to us at minecraft@staynalive.com and maybe we'll even join you for your presentation! Seriously — we think that would be *cool!*

» Obtaining obsidian and portals quickly

» Finding the right location to mine

» Following tips for avoiding overexertion

» Defeating basic mobs

» Obtaining experience points

» Figuring out how to craft quickly

» Taking inventory of basic equipment

» Finding natural comfort

Chapter **14**

Ten Helpful Survival Tips

Playing in Survival mode in Minecraft can be tough — even that first night can be hard to endure. Using just a few simple techniques, you can easily stay alive and survive, building your empire along the way. We wrote this chapter to help you through that survival process.

Dig Safely

Digging underground in Minecraft can be dangerous! Mine carefully to avoid these common hazards:

>> **Falling when digging straight down:** Breaking the block underneath you increases the danger of falling into a pit or a pool of lava. Staircase mines (described in Chapter 8) are useful because they don't require you to dig straight down.

>> **Falling sand and gravel or flowing lava when digging upward:** Quickly stop flowing lava with blocks such as cobblestone.

If you follow the safety tips we offer throughout this book, you can navigate dark caves and huge lava lakes with no problem.

Cook Efficiently

Sometimes you want to cook or smelt a large amount of material, such as beef to turn into steak or sand to burn into glass. Because you need a furnace and a plentiful source of fuel for this task, efficiently managing fuel is obviously an important skill.

You can cook with coal or any other hot or flammable material. Here are the best resources to use:

>> **Wooden plank:** Cooks 3 items for every 2 planks

>> **Coal:** Cooks 8 items per lump

>> **Blaze rod:** Cooks 12 items per rod

>> **Lava bucket:** Cooks 100 items

The latter two resources are useful only if you've spent time in the Nether — a dimension that can also provide a good source of coal, from wither skeletons, as described in Chapter 11.

In addition, you can cook one item using two saplings, so you can use saplings to your advantage if you don't need them for anything else. You can also cook an item with a wooden tool, providing a use for a neglected or near-broken wooden pickaxe.

TIP

You can also smelt wooden logs into charcoal, which is slightly more efficient — but more time-consuming — than converting them into planks. This trick is probably more useful for crafting torches and similar items.

Obtain Obsidian and Build Portals Quickly

If you're playing in Survival mode and you're itching to go to the Nether (you can find more information about it in Chapter 11), gather obsidian as fast as possible. Even if you can't find the diamond you need for a pickaxe, you can still build a portal if you can find some lava.

Simply use a bucket to place some still lava in the location where you want to place the obsidian, and then dump water over the lava to harden it. Use cobblestone or another nonflammable block to form a sort of mold for the portal and to form the container for the lava.

Mine in the Right Location

Denser ores such as redstone and diamond appear deep underground, but they're statistically common about three blocks above where bedrock spawns. This area is also abundant in lava, so be careful. To find a good spot to mine, you can dig down to this level: Either descend to bedrock and then move back up four blocks or press F3 in Java Edition, enable coordinates in Bedrock Edition, and dig until the y-coordinate is -57 — or find a sufficiently deep cave. Digging a tunnel stays more consistently at this depth, though a cave provides a larger surface area to search for minerals.

Avoid Overexertion

An action such as sprinting or jumping or suffering damage makes you hungry very quickly. Hunger can become irritating when you need a lot of food to stay on your feet. Follow these guidelines to avoid exerting yourself:

>> **Build roads with slabs and stairs.** These elements can help you move around without jumping.

>> **Connect your destinations with a minecart track.** This strategy is helpful if you must travel a long distance several times.

>> **If you're using a staircase mine, use actual stair blocks.** Then you can leave the mine without having to jump.

Defeat Basic Mobs

You must face zombies, spiders, creepers, and skeletons many times during your Minecraft experience. Each creature requires you to have a unique fighting style to defeat it. This list describes how to defeat each of these enemies (in order, from least to most threatening):

>> **Zombie:** Sprint and attack this enemy to knock it backward and then jump and attack repeatedly to drain its health. Knock back the closest ones to keep the shape of the group manageable.

>> **Spider:** Sprint-attack it! Try to predict a spider's jumps, and never let it gain the higher ground. Try to kill the spider quickly with a powerful sword because it has a low health level.

>> **Creeper:** Sprint and attack the creeper to prevent it from exploding near you. (It's extremely harmful.) If you don't care how you kill the creeper, try to lure it into exploding. If your timing is accurate, you can use creepers to destroy other pursuing mobs, especially spiders.

>> **Skeleton:** This archer works best alone. Try to situate yourself so that another mob is positioned between you and the skeleton — it sometimes shoots its own teammates! Use items such as blocks and trees to your advantage, by hiding behind them so that the skeleton must move close to you. If you're near a skeleton, simply kill it as fast as you can. Don't sprint-attack or else the skeleton gains more shooting space.

TIP

In addition, you can defeat many of these mobs easily by beating them into pits, cacti, or lava.

Obtain Experience Points

To advance into enchanting as you advance and explore the game, you need experience. Mobs, breeding, and mining any ores gives you experience. A helpful way to gain experience is to build an experience farm, also known as an XP farm or a Mob farm. (We don't cover that topic in this book, but you can find it on the Minecraft wiki by searching for *mob farm.*) *Experience farms* are farms you build to catch and store mobs, which you can easily attack to build up experience without incurring damage as you do so. Building experience farms may be a bit complicated, so we suggest mining for valuable minerals as an alternative.

We like to mine until we hit Level −57. On Levels 16 through −64, you can obtain diamonds in large numbers, and because your character is two blocks tall, you can mine at both Level −57 and Level −58. Levels 11 and lower are where lava lakes form. Stay away from lava lakes, and get the most out of your diamonds by creating enchantment tables, for example, which makes Levels −57 and −58 the places to gain the greatest amount of experience. You should strip-mine these two levels. Here's how:

1. **When you're at Level −57, mine horizontally for about 50 blocks.**

2. **Return to where you started and dig 3 blocks to the left of the tunnel you just mined.**

3. **On the third block, dig another 50 and then repeat this process.**

   Remember to mine the resources on the walls when you're done.

Light up tunnels to make sure that mobs don't spawn.

REMEMBER

Craft Quickly

You can craft material in several ways:

» **Notice what the game prompts you to do (Bedrock Edition).** Sometimes you halve an item, and sometimes you can quickly place items in, and remove them from, your inventory. Pay attention to what the game allows you to do.

» **Learn the ways of the hotkeys (Java Edition).** You can cut items in half by right-clicking on them. You can quickly put items in, and remove them from, the inventory by holding the Shift key and left-clicking. Or you can move an item to the hotbar by hovering the mouse cursor over the item and pressing the number on the keyboard that corresponds to the hotbar slot.

» **Craft several items at a time.** Figure 14-1 shows an efficient way to craft three tools at a time. When you take the axe, the remaining materials form a hoe and the layer beneath it forms a shovel.

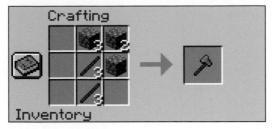

FIGURE 14-1: Crafting an axe, a hoe, and a shovel.

Check Basic Equipment

After playing Minecraft for a while and growing more confident in your ability to survive, you can store more items in the inventory and worry less about losing them. Then you can work more efficiently and return home less often.

Always carry in the inventory certain equipment and supplies on a Minecraft exploration — if you know how to keep them safe:

» **Food:** Carry food that you have an abundance of and that doesn't take up a lot of inventory space, such as bread or meat.

» **Weaponry:** Keep a sword ready, and possibly a bow or armor. Place a sword in the first slot of the inventory so that you can access it by pressing the 1 key.

» **Pickaxe, axe, and shovel:** Gathering materials while you're exploring is always useful, and if you ever need to break a block, you should have the proper tool ready, for efficiency's sake. A pickaxe is vital in underground areas.

» **Torch:** Never go mining without several torches to light the area.

Find Natural Comfort

If you need shelter before dark in the hills or the jungle for safety overnight, find an enclosed area (a shallow cave, natural copse, or large tree, for example), and fill in the cracks with blocks to turn it into a natural-looking house.

Glossary

biome: A region that has distinct geographical features. For example, grass changes color depending on the biome. Biomes, which are all distinct, are used to break up the world with forests and deserts, for example.

bedrock (the block): The only naturally generated, unbreakable block that lines the floor of the Overworld and the roof and floor of the Nether.

craft: To create a new item. On a crafting menu, you combine various items in a specific way, known as a recipe, to create a new item. In the inventory, you have a small, 2x2 crafting area used to make basic items, though most items are crafted using a crafting table.

creative mode: A Minecraft mode, accessible only in a creative world or in a world where commands are allowed, in which you have the ability to fly and get any block in the game and you cannot take damage. One of four modes in Minecraft, this one is perfect for planning builds beforehand, or for just experimenting with Minecraft.

creeper: A hostile mob (the most famous mob in pop culture) that blows up if it gets close enough to you. It sneaks up behind you or falls in front of you, if it gets the opportunity, to ensure a sneaky, creepy kill. See Chapter 2.

drop: An item that a mob or another players lets go of (or "drops") when they die. It is commonly spoken of this way: "What are the drops for a pig?" or "Look at what the wither dropped!"

enchant: To use the enchanting table block on an item. An enchant is a modifier to that item, commonly used on armor to get a "protection" enchant, which increases the level of damage that piece of armor blocks. Enchants also create a shimmering effect to that item.

endermen: Another popular mob in Minecraft is the enderman, based on the Slenderman game (a horror game where you would run from a slender, faceless creature, that if you looked at, you would die). If you look at the enderman, it becomes enraged and will attack you relentlessly while teleporting to create a sporadic attack pattern. Endermen can also pick up blocks and move them around.

entity: Any nonstatic item in the game. For example, all mobs are entities, as are dropped items, item frames, and ignited TNT. Entities can be anything as long as they have some changing property.

grief: To destroy, pillage, and/or plunder someone's items or base, for example. *Griefer* is the term used for someone who griefs.

hunger bar: The bar, which looks like half-eaten meat directly above the hotbar, that indicates how "hungry" you are. The more bars that are gone, the hungrier you are. If the bar depletes to three bars or fewer, you can no longer sprint, and if it depletes to zero, you start taking damage to a certain amount, depending on the game difficulty.

mine: To search and collect resources found underground. When you mine for iron, you go underground to search for and collect iron.

mob: A *mob*ile entity, or a sentient entity, that moves around and often interacts with the world. Common mobs are animals, monsters, and pets.

Nether: A lava-filled, fiery, hell-like dimension filled with a red-colored block known as netherrack. The Nether features some of the scariest mobs in.

Overworld: A unique location, containing diverse biomes and underground systems, where you most often play the game. In the Overworld, you spawn and enter portals to the other dimensions.

smelt: To melt an ore or a raw material and turn it into an ingot, by using a blast furnace or a regular furnace.

SMP (Survival MultiPlayer): A world in which everyone is in Survival mode, but also in a multiplayer world, so that more than one person at a time can play on it.

sneak: An action bound to a button. When you hold down that button, your character crouches, causing you to move slower and quieter and hiding your nametag from other people on a multiplayer server. If you're holding sneak, you're also prevented from moving off the edge of a block.

sprint: A way to move faster than walking speed. Though this action is bound to a button, you can instead quickly move forward twice. Though you are moving faster, the hunger bar is also depleted faster than normal.

Survival mode: The most common mode in Minecraft, and the one this book focuses on. In Survival mode, you see the hunger bar, the health bar, and the mobs that want to attack you. In this mode, you must hunt and gather resources to advance in the game.

The End: The dimension where the ender dragon (the final boss of the game) lies, and one filled with endermen and a sandy-colored stone, known as end stone. After you defeat the dragon, you can traverse to the far ends of The End, to end cities, where you can find special items such as shulker boxes.

Index

About the Authors

Jesse Stay is a web and social media expert and the author of 11 books, including one of the first published books about Facebook, the first book about Facebook application development, and, most recently, one of the first published books about TikTok. Jesse is an accomplished and world-renowned speaker, and an all-around expert in technology, especially in the areas of digital and social media and social media marketing (Facebook and Myspace are former clients of his!).

Jesse eats, breathes, and sleeps the web, TikTok, Facebook, Twitter, and other future-leaning and connecting technologies. In addition to this book, he wrote *Minecraft For Dummies,* and *Minecraft Recipes For Dummies* (all published by Wiley) with three of his sons: Thomas, Joseph, and Alexander. Jesse believes strongly in using technology as a tool to unite the entire family, and he believes that Minecraft is one of the best tools to do it.

Jesse spends his spare time as a single dad with his seven kids (whenever they'll give him the time). His most recent passions as a newly single dad (outside of TikTok, of course) are digging into the data behind dating apps, comprehending the psychology and dynamics of relationships, and teaching other men how to become better men from his studies. He is also <ahem> a newly minted Bitcoin and cryptocurrency nerd.

If any of these topics piques your interest, you can find Jesse at his own website (http://jessestay.com) or email him at jesse@staynalive.com.

Joseph Stay, at age 17, wrote most of this book! He is Jesse's son, who, while writing this book, also just finished his first year of college. Joseph is studying computer engineering and is taking an interest in network engineering. He loves to work on his custom mechanical keyboards and program on the side. He also loves to make YouTube videos, like ones you can find at https://www.youtube.com/user/minecraftdummiesbook. Joseph hopes to write more books, like his father does. He's also looking for coding and networking jobs to support his schooling — reach out to him at josephhstay@gmail.com or at the address in Jesse's bio if you'd like Joseph to work for you!

Dedication

From Jesse: All of these books, and my entire career, are for my kids, and their bright futures. All seven of you. You know who you are. You are my everything.

From Joseph: To Technoblade, the man whose achievements go beyond anything I could say — a legend living amongst mere mortals and the man who can never, truly die.

Authors' Acknowledgments

As always, thanks to all the staff at Wiley and all those who worked with us on this book — many we don't even have the names for, but would include here if we did. Thanks especially to our project editor, Tracy Brown Hamilton, for probably one of the easiest and most straightforward editing processes we've experienced so far; our technical editor, James Hunt; Lindsay Lefevere, who made the next edition of our *Minecraft For Dummies* world become reality; as well as our book agent, Carole Jelen, for helping us along the way. We couldn't have written this book without any of you.

Publisher's Acknowledgments

Acquisitions Editor: Lindsay Lefevere

Project Editor: Tracy Brown

Copy Editor: Rebecca Whitney

Technical Editor: James Hunt

Production Editor: Mohammed Zafar Ali

Cover Image: Courtesy of Joseph Stay and Alexander Stay